RISK FOR FREEDOM

ONE FAMILY'S QUEST

George Stastny

STASTNY

FREEDOM
PUBLISHING

Risk For Freedom
One Family's Quest
by George Stastny

Stastny Freedom Publishing
9870 SW Bayou Drive
McMinnville, OR 97128-8601   USA
www.riskforfreedom.net
orders: info@riskforfreedom.net

Cover design drawn by George Stastny
Photograph of the author by Tom Ballard
Printed by Print NW, McMinnville, Oregon

Publisher's Cataloging-in-Publication
(Provided by Quality Books, Inc.)
Stastny, George J. (George Joseph)
Risk For Freedom: One Family's Quest / George J. Stastny.
p.cm.

LCCN 2009911067
ISBN-13: 978-0-9843132-2-8
ISBN-10: 0-0943132-2-2
1. Stastny, George J. (George Joseph). 2. Stastny, George J. (George Joseph)—Family. 3. Czechs—United States—Biography.
4. Immigrants—United States—Biography. 5. Czech Americans—Biography. 6. Artists—Biography. I. Title

E184.B67S73 2010   973'.049186'0092   QBI09-600199

I would like to dedicate this book to two friends who are very important in my life. They were very helpful, thoughtful and generous to my family and me when I came to the United States.

From the bottom of my heart, with love, to Cleo and Ed Tomco.

TABLE OF CONTENTS

Acknowledgements

I would like to express my deepest thanks to my wife, Carolyn, for the endless encouragement and support that she has given me from the very beginning of our relationship. She performed better than a stepmother to our children; she became a real loving and caring mom. I also treasure when she always shows spontaneously her happiness for any of my successes and achievements. In putting this book together, she gave me so much encouragement and dedicated endless months of hard work. She helped so much that I hope I can thank her enough.

I need to thank my new friend, Melissa Bernhardt. She is the person who generated the idea to write this book, and she is actually responsible for me not forgetting this idea or sweeping it under the carpet. I put the manuscript on the back burner so many times, but she never gave up and kept encouraging me to continue and finish it. She made me believe that I am capable, not just to tell my story, but to put it into writing. Melissa, thank you very much for your tireless encouragement, professional knowledge, enthusiasm, endless and generous help, and true friendship.

I also want to thank my friend and respected photographer, Tom Ballard, for his expertise and generous help with all the digital graphic needs of this book. He spent days on his computer, doctoring my old and sometimes damaged photographs and adjusting my drawings that I needed to use, preparing all of them for printing.

Foreword

I am one of those readers who believe every aspect of a book contributes to the total experience. I read everything in a book – the introduction and preface, to get an understanding of the author's motivations and purposes, the dedication, acknowledgements, dust jacket, and author biography. For me, all of this information provides important context for the actual text. It is in that vein that I offer this introduction – and most likely for that reason that George Stastny asked me to write it.

I am neither famous nor any sort of literary critic. I am not mentioned once in the story of George's life. I am simply one person who heard his story, found it inspiring, and doggedly encouraged him to share it with others.

George and I met in the summer of 2003, when both of our families were vacationing in Canada. My husband and sons were off enjoying a day in the mountains, and I decided to take a leisurely stroll around Lake Louise. Coffee in hand, I set out for what I expected to be a quiet twenty-minute walk. Along the way, I met George and his wife, Carolyn, and began what I thought would be a polite chat. Hearing his accent I asked about his background. What started as a short walk became a six and a half hour hike up a glacier. During our walk, we had focused entirely on one topic – his life. I was completely captivated by his story and his family's harrowing escape from communist Czechoslovakia in 1980. I was intrigued by the history, the politics, the psychology and the principles. Our ages were separated by only 12 years; yet our lives had been so vastly different. As I listened to his story, I continually tried to relate my life to his. As fascinated as I was by the facts, I found myself wondering how I would have responded to the same set of circumstances and risks. I wondered whether I knew anyone who could have, or would have, responded with George's courage and resourcefulness. I asked countless questions about the emotional, physical, and financial toil of his life under communist control, the motivations and logistics of his escape through the Iron Curtain, and the difficulties and opportunities of his new life in America.

The more I asked, the more George talked. The more George talked, the further we hiked… After the first few hours, I realized that my fascination extended beyond the facts and the related psychology. There was something more that kept me trudging up that glacier. I came to realize that he was sharing his story with an unusually keen recall of details, the descriptiveness of an artist, and a unique willingness to share a broad range of emotions with a perfect stranger. It was this rare combination of history, psychology and emotion which captivated me.

In a moment of unusual conviction, I asked George and Carolyn if we could work together to ensure his story was preserved for others to share. We initially considered a variety of options for the book format and, after much deliberation, elected to go with the medium which felt most natural – a conversation. My family and I traveled to their home in Oregon in 2005, and began our project with a lengthy recording of George's life journey. We were his guests and listened intently as he again shared the details of his unique and inspiring life. After several years and countless edits, his story has now been printed for all to share. Our sincere hope is that as you read the following pages you will also feel like you are George's guest. While he has worked tirelessly to ensure historical accuracy and to provide helpful transitions, his book is neither expertly polished nor scripted. It is as if he were speaking directly to you. We have intentionally kept the text closely aligned with the original recording – hoping that his syntax and cadence will add to the experience.

As you read his story, I believe you will find yourself marveling at his determination, priorities, ingenuity, and good humor. I think you will find more than just an interesting story about a man's life. I believe you will find a variety of themes engaging your mind and your emotions. And, for those who gained American citizenship by birth, you may find yourself with a renewed appreciation for your good fortune.

Melissa Bernhardt

Atlanta, GA

Some Key Names

Jaroslav Stastny	George's older brother
Louie Rychtarik	George's lifetime friend – from birth through today. Born in the same place in the same week.
Helena	George's first wife
George, Jr.	First son
Martin	Second son
Simon	One of George's closest friends in Czechoslovakia.
Vasek Suda	Friend in Czechoslovakia who helped with house
Jaroslav Zeman	Trusted friend and partner on the crane
Josef	Official who helped with escape
Vasek Schuster	Czech immigrant living in Vienna
Cleo and Ed Tomco	U.S. sponsors for Stastny family
Ivan Votava	Owner of special flag
Carolyn	George's current wife
Note:	"Jaroslav" and "Vasek" are common Czech names. You will read them more than once.

Preface

First, I have to introduce myself. I am George Stastny, living in McMinnville, Oregon. I was born in Prague, Czechoslovakia, on April 1, 1944. My wife Carolyn says it fits me perfectly to be an "April Fool!" When I was 36 years old, I escaped with the whole family – two boys, Martin, age seven and George, Jr., age nine and my first wife Helena – from communist Czechoslovakia through the Iron Curtain to the United States. That is easy to say, but it took quite a bit of time to go through this process of escaping and starting my new life in the United States.

I'm not a book writer, not even a very good book reader. I don't have any experience in this field. My new friend, Melissa Bernhardt from Atlanta, Georgia, approached me after hearing my life story and encouraged me to write this book. I didn't believe that I would be capable of writing a book, knowing that it would be done in a very amateur way. And because English is my second language, learned later in life as an adult, it would be full of mistakes. I also knew it would be emotionally draining to relive all the details of my experience as I told the story. However, Melissa and my wife Carolyn assured me that the readers would overlook the problems with my grammar and occasional emotional moments and be able to focus on the themes and message of my story. I hope they are correct. They also convinced me that I could do this in spite of the geographic distance between Oregon and Georgia. As time progressed, I gained confidence in my ability to finish this project. Melissa and Carolyn helped so much and they really deserve the biggest compliment.

I would like to share this story with you to emphasize the beautiful value of freedom that comes with citizenship in the United States. I think I have a unique perspective of what freedom means – and what it is worth. I honestly believe that freedom is worth the risk, many times worth the risk, of everything else that seems important to you.

Please make yourselves comfortable and thank you for reading my story.

1

Basic Information About Czechoslovakia

S ince many people who have heard my story are interested in history, culture, etc., I feel it would not hurt to refresh the memories of readers with a little basic background and facts about Czechoslovakia. I think this might actually be helpful.

Czechoslovakia was created on October 28, 1918, out of two nations, and for that reason the name of the country is "Czech" and "Slovakia" put together as "Czech-o-Slovakia." For simplicity, just think of the "o" meaning "and." The country is exactly in the geographic center of Europe, surrounded

Central Europe before Germany was divided – 1945

before WWII by Poland, Russia, Hungary, Austria, and Germany. All of Czechoslovakia is about the same size as the state of New York with the same population of around 15 million. Even though Czechoslovakia is now Czech Republic and Slovakia, two separate countries, you will still hear from me "Czechoslovakia" and I mean it that way, because that was the time in our history when I was born, lived there and escaped from there.

The capitol is Prague with a population of 1½ million. That's where I'm from. The historical center of Prague is a well-preserved, unique, beautiful and charming city that became very popular after the fall of communism for tourists from all over the world. As of 2008, over 50,000 Americans live in Prague, having fallen in love with the city and its lifestyle – and with the pretty girls and the beer – in my opinion! Prague has very sophisticated public transportation, including buses, streetcars and a great network of subways. Building a subway in Prague was not easy. It's easier to build a subway system on flat terrain, but Prague is anything but flat. This project faced many challenges – tunneling through hills and under a major river, not to mention the fact that part of the city sits on sand. Historical buildings include museums, cathedrals, churches, theaters, and concert halls that host music festivals from all over the world. Prague is a mecca for musicians and

My picture of Prague from Charles Bridge taken in late 1970's

is simply a place with a long cultural tradition and connection to the arts, sports and industry.

Czechoslovakia was always an economically developed and advanced country, one of the top ten in the world, prior to the takeover after WWII led by the communists in Moscow. At one time, the country was ranked economically number two in the world. Because of its own natural resources and climate, agriculture was very well developed, as was steel because of coal and metal ore. Light cars, heavy trucks, trains, airplanes – all were produced in our country from this ore. Three large automobile manufacturers – Skoda, Tatra and Praga – made many different models of passenger cars, light and heavy trucks, and military vehicles. These companies also produced machinery and equipment for other industries such as agriculture, sugar mills, steel mills, coal mines, railroads, chemical and petroleum plants, etc. There were large coal mines and steel mills in Kladno and Ostrava. Famous motorcycles (Jawa and CZ) were made in Strakonice, firearms by Zbrojovka in Brno. A huge foundry (CKD) making anything out of cast iron was located in Prague. Tesla made electronic appliances and equipment. Dental and medical equipment were produced by Chirana. And of course, everyone knows about the superior glass making, all kinds of glass, especially beautiful Bohemian cut crystal glassware and chandeliers as well as Moser glass. Famous porcelain china was produced in Karlovy Vary. Beer production, the best in the world – the first lager in the world was created in Plzen (Pilsen in English) as well as Budvar (Budweiser). Since beer is considered the national drink, there are countless numbers of large breweries throughout the whole country. String and brass music instruments, pianos (Petrof) made in Hradec Kralove, and countless factories producing furniture, textiles, paper, toys, light bulbs, soaps, matches, etc., etc. Czechoslovakia also made many cultural contributions to fine art as well as classical music from such famous composers as Dvorak, Smetana, and Janacek. Hydroelectric dams around the world use Czech-invented Kaplan turbines. This is just a small sampling of what this country was producing. I am very proud to describe Czechoslovakia in this shining light, but I need to remind you again, that this is a picture of the country prior to the time when communists took over and put into place their socialistic ideas. After you have heard my story, you will understand more of what happened as a result of this takeover.

Now that you know a little bit about Czechoslovakia, you would like me to start to answer the basic question, "Why and how did you escape?" Because of the complexity of the story, I also need to prepare you for jumping from one subject to another, from one time period to another, but please pay attention and be patient, because eventually, everything will tie together. I will try my best.

Living under the communist government was at a certain point hard, but not so hard if you were born under communism. You wouldn't know anything better. I was born in 1944, almost at the end of WWII. The war ended in 1945 and at that time Czechoslovakia became free again, but only for a short time. I still remember when I was 4 years old, that my father had a very productive tailoring business. My mother had plenty of money to buy food, everyday supplies and much more. Our family was very happy and successful as were all of our neighbors and relatives, but this rapidly slowed down because in 1948, Czechoslovakia came under the influence of the Soviet Union, in other words, Russia.

Happy family under the Christmas tree. From left: Brother Jaroslav, Mother Milada, Father Jaroslav, myself

And so, from early childhood, when I was only four years old, I remember communism as a part of my life, home and lifestyle. I was very lucky as a child to have a loving family who surrounded and protected me from what was happening to our country politically. My parents were providing for me and my brother the maximum – love, care, a clean home, good food (as good as my mother could make with limited supply), and a high standard of morality. However, as I was getting older, I began to understand that the communists kept information about the rest of the world away from us. But people of the older generation, of course, had experienced and remembered freedom. They couldn't be fooled. And then there were some other leakages of information about what the real free world looked like. Some prominent and lucky people traveled to other countries in the free part of the world. And they brought some information back to us. Most of these people were scientists attending symposiums, performing artists, or competing athletes. These people found out what life looked like in the free part of the world. We found out that stores in the West were fully stocked with goods and that an ordinary person's paycheck was enough to live on comfortably. We were living under a corrupt regime with shortages of everyday supplies. As an adult, in order to provide for my own family, I always had to zigzag through the system. These reasons were not why I escaped. I escaped for different reasons. This story is very complex and after reading it, you will find out what those reasons were. But for now, to explain briefly, the bottom line for me was freedom.

7

2

Early Childhood

I think that under communism we had a very good education. I received good schooling and I was raised in a family that I respected, appreciated, and honored. I had good family values – knowing what was right and wrong – and I was surrounded with love. When I was in school my friendship with other kids was very good. Our friendship between the neighbors was also very good. But there was always something that as a child I was taught from a very, very early age. "George, what you hear at home, you don't say in school or in front of some people that you don't know anything about. You can talk with very good friends only. There are some questionable subjects that you can talk about only at home." It was very dangerous to talk against the regime. In the school, for instance, it would have been a disaster for my parents, for my whole family, if I had said something critical against the regime.

I remember times in the late 40's and early 50's when we were not allowed to listen to some radio stations. These stations were broadcasting from Germany and Austria. They were called "Radio Free Europe" and "The Voice of America." My father was listening to these stations in our home under a blanket – a well-padded blanket. And he had the radio on very low under that blanket, so no neighbors would hear it. Listening to news broadcasts and getting information from these two stations was more than getting a second opinion. It was a kind of assurance and confirmation of what my father and millions of people like him already knew or guessed. They knew that communist radio stations were lying, twisting the truth, denying the facts, promising many things that they couldn't deliver and would never happen. The communists also called the free stations "hate radio and Western propaganda." Actually, both sides hated each other and called each other liars, but for ordinary people living under the new communist rules, for people who just lost their opportunity to be really free, it was so obvious who was right and who was wrong and who was closer to the truth. Being able to listen to these broadcasts lasted for only a few years because the communists were furious that their lies were being questioned and proved wrong. It didn't take too long before "scramblers" were installed all over the city and the populated countryside, so that it became impossible to listen to these favorite free radio stations.

So, I grew up in this kind of fear on one side, and on the other side in the school, newspapers and on the local radios, we heard how free we were and how lucky we were that the communists were taking such good care of us. They were bragging about how much freedom we had. But this was freedom only to a certain point. For instance, I could choose sports if I wanted to. I could choose hobbies to a certain point. And as a teenager I remember I had so many hobbies. I was very much into the arts, sports, dancing, music, and building things.

I was lucky I had an older brother, Jaroslav, who was six years older and had more skills and a wider range of interests. He was better in some hobbies and later, as I grew up, I was better in some others. And we were helping each other. For instance, when he was a teenager, he was the one who was starting to play guitar, and I was the one who started photography. I was eight or nine years old. Later, at one point he proposed, " How about you teach me how to take and develop pictures, and I will teach you how to play the guitar." Over a number of years, I think I became a better guitar player, and he became a better photographer. Sometimes we still tease each other about that.

We fought quite a bit just like any other brothers, but we also spent a lot of good times together. Since he was older, I learned a lot from him, a lot about various tools, especially hand tools. He was excellent at explaining mechanics and physics to me. I have to give him credit for his patience with me, and I hope that I didn't slow him down too much in his own development. One Christmas our parents gave him an Erector Set and he made many things out of it. They were too complicated for me, but I started to play with this set at a very early age and was making simple creations out of it. Gradually I progressed into more complicated pieces; my favorite ones were cars, trucks and cranes.

When my brother was about 11, it was very obvious to my parents that, in order to keep developing his skills, he needed more room and some kind of a little shop where he would have his own space. He had so many hand tools including a little three-inch vise but nowhere to attach it. Our apartment wasn't very big, and I still remember the exact layout. From the entry you walked into the hallway with five more doors – one into the kitchen, one into the bedroom that was also the living room, one into the toilet room, one into the bathtub room, and one into a very small pantry/storage room. Our parents emptied this little storage room and gave it to Jaroslav so he could create a miniature shop there. It was really cool that my parents did that. Jaroslav immediately built a workbench, and a bunch of shelves with brackets and hooks for his hand tools. After all that, there was room for only one chair.

I loved to squeeze behind my brother's chair, standing there, looking over his shoulder and learning always something new. He made so many things there from scratch, such as a perfect scale model of a trolley bus about nine inches long (the city was installing a new line of trolley buses at that time). This model had a 12-volt motor, front wheels that steered, working headlights and tail lights. It was awesome. He made many models of glider planes and as he was growing up and getting older, he started more and more with electronics. He made from scratch an amplifier, a radio, a tape deck, a turntable with an exchanger for playing ten records, an electric pickup for a guitar, a steel or Hawaiian guitar which he started to learn how to play. When we got older, we also collected many music instruments and learned how to play them. Of course, our first performances were not very ear-pleasing. We liked to pretend we were having a real concert. Some neighbors were tolerant and some hated us! I also liked to build little rigs with old ice skates attached underneath. This very popular toy that we called a "little bob" was something to sit on and slide on icy downhills in the winter. My friends and I could hardly wait to get out of school so we could hit the hills and race each other until dark. In the summer I made a slightly different, slightly larger rig and attached wheels so I could run down hills on pavement. These were very primitive toys, but very popular among the kids and we had a lot of fun with them. I guess you could say that these rigs were pioneers to today's skateboards, but we could only go downhill and we sat on them.

When I was a little kid, the small businesses in the neighborhood were still trying to be productive and hadn't yet been harassed and seized by communists. I felt lucky living in a neighborhood where people were so talented and skilled. As a little boy, I was going from shop to shop, watching workers and craftsmen creating different things. Imagine watching people making beautiful furniture from scratch, welding sidecars for motorcycles, fixing cars and bicycles, or being in the knife sharpening shop where my father had all his scissors sharpened. My father had a friend who was an architect who designed new types of windows using multi-functional hinges. I think I learned a lot from him about drawing and drafting. I also learned drawing from my parents who were both good at that. One Christmas they gave me a beautiful wooden case full of drawing supplies – watercolors, brushes, colored pencils and inks, etc. I was so happy I felt like I was in heaven! I used this artist's kit a lot. There were a couple of artists, husband and wife, in our building. She was a painter and he was a sculptor. I was always fascinated by their work. Since that time I always wanted to be a sculptor. I dreamt about that but I also thought that this dream was too high and not realistic.

I had a friend, a girl, whose name was Dana. Her mom and grandparents were photographers. They had a very large apartment that they turned into a photo studio with its own dark room. Dana and I played together a lot, and I was in their home, studio and the dark room every day. That was most likely the place where my love for photography started. Dana's mother took many pictures of us. One time we were teasing her that we will get married (we were five years old!) and she said, "OK!" She dressed us up as a bride and groom, put us in front of their big studio camera and took a picture.

My first wedding picture! Dana and myself – five years old

I still have that picture and many others that she took. For me, growing up surrounded by all these little businesses, including my father's tailor shop, was such a good and valuable learning experience. But unfortunately, with communism taking over the whole country, these valuable small businesses and shops gradually disappeared. What a loss and waste for future generations!

When we were getting older and we were starting to think about what we were going to do with our lives, what we were going to do for a living, we were not so free. Then I saw a lot of differences and favoring students who were from communist families. For them, the doors to colleges were wide open. For students who were not from communist families, it was a lot more difficult to get into any higher education school. For them to be admitted, they had to be very gifted and have only excellent grades. Average students didn't stand a chance.

Let me mention some important facts about communist politics. Pictures celebrating Russians were everywhere. Pictures and statues of only Russians liberating Czechoslovakia were in the schools, parks, public offices and places, even in the windows of some stores. Ironically, sometimes these stores didn't have enough food, but they still had pictures of Russians. The communists totally denied that, in 1945, Czechoslovakia was liberated also from the West by American troops led by Gen. Patton. What a ridiculously transparent communist lie! Everybody knew the truth, but we were not allowed to say it. The communists constantly tried to get us to believe we were liberated completely and only by the Russians. Because of propaganda and favoring only one side, the communists left out, on purpose, the Americans in stories of our liberation. They created new textbooks and changed history as a result. If my father had walked into the school and said to teachers, "Hey, you guys are teaching the wrong thing," then that would have been the end to our happy family. But my father told us the real true story at home. We talked about these things quite openly in our family, but we had been instructed by our parents for our safety NOT TO TELL ANYBODY! I will give more attention to this subject about our liberation later.

Fifth grade, 1955 – Louie on top row, 4th from left, myself directly below Louie

Here I have a picture from fifth grade, and you can see how many children came from communist families. Those kids are wearing white shirts with red scarves and blue pants or skirts which was the indication that they were being prepared for potential membership in the Communist Party.

The communists started to brainwash children from an early age. They called those little ones (starting in the first grade), "Sparks." Then later on (in the fifth grade – eighth grade), they called these kids "Pioneers." So the kids in this picture are the Pioneers. You can see who was from a communist family and who was not. Those who were not would just have on normal ordinary street clothes. You can see me right here. I don't have the communist uniform. Here in the same picture, you see my best friend, Louie Rychtarik, also in normal clothes. I must tell you much more about Louie.

Louie and I are lifetime friends. We were born in the same place almost at the same time. Louie is only one week younger than me. We grew up together, went through all levels of our education together. We did so many things together through our childhood and our youth. We got into so much mischief that it could be a book by itself. I want to prepare you that you will hear about Louie many more times. Our families were close and in the same situation. We had a lot less than the communist kids. They had the new bicycles and the good toys. They had better apartments, even houses, and cars. My parents never had a car. Louie's parents never had a car either. Under communism, my parents were, I would say, poor for most of their lives. I was the first one in the family to eventually have a car when I became an adult, 21 years old. Of course, it was an old clunker. I had to work on it all the time to keep it running, but it was a CAR!

Let me tell you a little bit about my first bicycle. This was a bicycle that was in the attic of a neighbor of my grandparents, who lived in the country. I was there on summer vacation visiting my grandma and grandpa, and I was fixing bicycles in the neighborhood for other people, but I never had my own bike. One day, one of those neighbors said, "George, we have an old bicycle in the attic, if you would be interested in looking at it and maybe have it." I was so excited. I was probably 12 – 13 years old. I got it out of the cobwebs and washed it. It was a very old bike, kind of old-fashioned, totally out of style with very large and flat tires, but I saw immediately a lot of potential in it. I was so excited, and so I fixed it, but then I had a problem. I was 50 miles or so from our home in Prague, and I had to notify my parents that I would be coming home with a bicycle. I wrote and sent a letter to them, asking if I can have an old but BEAUTIFUL bike. I needed to ask for this because we didn't have room for it in our apartment in Prague. My heart was just pounding hoping that they would say, "yes." The answer came back kind of positive. They didn't want to break my heart, I guess. So I brought this bike to our home in Prague. I took it apart, cleaned and fixed everything on it, and I repainted it. I was so proud and I thought I had a pretty cool-looking bike. It had looked like an old clunker and now it looked really decent. Much later, I did the same thing with motorcycles and later with cars. Other kids had little motorcycles (only 50 or 60 cubic centimeters) and they didn't know how to work on them. Some kids didn't even have drivers' licenses and their parents, who were communists, had money to buy all these toys and goodies for them. I had a driver's license and I knew how to fix these vehicles, but I couldn't buy any of these. I was always very happy when somebody would let me use his or her toy around the block. Some kid would get a new motorcycle and wouldn't even know how to drive it home from the store. So they would ask me to do it for them. That was an exciting opportunity again for me to ride a small motorcycle.

3

Nationalizing Businesses and Coercing Party Membership

In the early 50's, if we as children were to have said something against the regime in the school or in the wrong place, our parents would have been persecuted. Because we were very careful and lucky, we were not caught. But nevertheless, my father was the victim of the communists nationalizing small businesses.

Before WWII, Czechoslovakia was free, and my father started his successful custom tailoring business. Then we were occupied by Germans. Very shortly after the war, but before the Russians took us over, we were free for about three years. Between the end of the war in 1945 and the communist takeover in 1948, I still remember as a little child that my father was making enough money to support our family. He was taking courses for his driver's license because he wanted to buy a car. I don't know how many people could afford to buy a car in the U.S. in 1945, but in Czechoslovakia, only people who were well off could do so. He also wanted to buy a house and some vacation property. I was a little boy and I was growing up in this environment. We were free and everything was fine. My father was a respected tailor, very skilled. He was not the type of tailor who would be putting patches on knees or the elbows of jackets. He was doing custom designs, his own designs, for very high class clients. Lawyers, doctors, architects, etc. He would take the measurements and ask, "Would you like a pocket here? How about a collar? Cuffs? Stripes? That would look very elegant." He took a flat piece of fabric and sculpted it into a three-dimensional form to fit each individual perfectly. To me he was an artist/sculptor in fabric.

When the communists took over in 1948, they stole, literally stole, all big businesses and industries. Steel mills, coal mines, big factories, etc. And they didn't give anybody any choice. Let's say they took over an automobile factory. They needed the workers because the workers knew how to produce automobiles. They kept those workers in place. They told the owner of this factory, "You are going to work for us on the floor somewhere – maybe pushing a broom – or you are going to be in jail." So this owner didn't really have a choice. It was unbelievable. Can you imagine how he felt? He had started this factory and it took him many years to develop it to a prosperous stage. This factory was his property, and the communists just stole it from him. There were a lot of people, smart people, who didn't even care about negotiating. They knew that they would never go for this rotten deal, pushing a broom. So they escaped from the country – to some free countries. It was very hard for them to leave behind everything they had accomplished. At that time there was no Iron Curtain so it was easier. We will talk about that later.

Many escaped to Canada and the United States. Most of them, because they were in the prime time of their lives and because they had the skills, were able to start again. For example there is a company now in Canada, called Bata, which was a Czech shoe company that was the first shoe company in the world to begin making shoes on an assembly line. That owner escaped to Canada and started over. So to explain this more, when these owners left, the communists put their own people into the management positions. This was the beginning of a very corrupt system of putting family members and friends into high positions. These new communist "managers" didn't have any experience running those factories. They didn't know anything about anything. They were just communists.

The factory was still producing automobiles or shoes because the workers knew how to make them. The communists forgot a very important thing – you can't have a person in a leadership position who has only a party badge and no knowledge of how to lead and be an expert. A good business leader must be a person who is knowledgeable, motivated and dedicated. Without these characteristics, business will go downhill and there is no other way. And sure enough, the factories were slowly going downhill instead of producing more and more, instead of making new models, better products, and improving technologies. Instead, they were making more and more mistakes. And that's how it worked from 1948. And the only thing the communists were good at was bragging that they nationalized the businesses. They were also trumpeting to the whole world how good they were, how much they were achieving, always breaking production records of their hypothetical five-year economic plans. They created an illusion around themselves and as a result, 20 years later we were driving plastic two-cycle cars with a polluting engine smaller than a riding lawn mower. These "cars" were very cheaply made in East Germany and called "Trabant."

By the way, Czech people, even under hard times and stress, always kept a good spirit and sense of humor. There was a joke going around about these plastic "cars":

One fellow was asking another, "Do you know that Americans are ordering a large number of these Trabants?" The other fellow replied, "Really?" "Yeah, they want to use them in their big Cadillacs as ash trays!"

There was another big problem because, as everybody knows, small businesses are as important as big businesses – and maybe even more. Without these little businesses, there wouldn't be any competition. Competition is extremely important for the economy and very healthy for consumers. But that didn't bother the communists. They didn't want to have any competition.

It was very difficult for the communists to take over small businesses because they didn't have anybody to put into the shoes of these little business owners. My father as a tailor didn't have any employees. He had two sewing machines. He had needles, thread, fabric, and leather. But the most important thing was that he had the knowledge, skills and experience. He was dedicated to his business and he worked very hard. He was holding onto his business, and the communists couldn't say, "Give us your business. We will put somebody in your place. We will use your two sewing machines." They wouldn't have anything without my father. They needed him. My father was the business. It was very difficult for communists to convince my father and people like him that they should give up their businesses and work for the regime. And I need to say, my father was one of the hardest ones to give up.

It was also very difficult when communists started to talk to farmers. Farmers are very much attached to their land. They feel like their land is their blood and body. You cannot take land from the farmer. And that is what the communists were doing. They didn't have much without the farmer. They needed the farmer with the land. What they ended up doing turned very ugly. In some cases, they were killing farmers because the farmers refused to budge. It was like in the movie, "The Magnificent Seven." You see the farmer take the hoe and run against someone who has a gun. There is no chance. Later the government made these farms "collective farms."

There used to be borders between properties, but the communists didn't care. They just plowed everything together. First of all they messed up the wildlife because the wild rabbits and birds didn't have a place to hide. Everything looked like an airport – flat for miles and miles. They didn't think about irrigating, so it was dry. They were producing very little. And working for communists was not as attractive, as motivating, as working for yourself. The work ethic of these collective "farmers" was terrible. There was a joke about it. I remember that they came to work, they were sitting from morning in the tavern drinking beer and saying, "The fields are still too wet." They slowly got drunk. In the afternoon they started to say, "Oh, the fields are too dry!" And then they went home and nothing was done. When farmers work for themselves, they work hard from very early until late at night. They always think about their property and their livestock first and second about themselves. To have your own business or farm is a big obligation. If you don't want to fail, you MUST take care of your business now! You cannot kid yourself by saying, "I'll do it later." The word "later" should not even be in your vocabulary. When it's time to irrigate, you must irrigate. Plants must be watered otherwise they will die. The same with the livestock. There is a time to feed, to milk, time to clean, etc. If you work for a government farm, you are not as motivated and you might think that you can be late, that somebody else will do it. But that somebody else is thinking the same way and the result is, "Oh well. We didn't produce anything. It's not mine anyway."

Let's talk about my father and people like him. The communists were trying to get their businesses and they couldn't convince them. So, they put very high taxes on their incomes. It didn't help. People were working harder and harder. My father was paying taxes equal to half of his income. It came to the point where people were hiding income or cheating to be able to survive. It was very difficult to control them. Things went so far that taxes were almost equal to the income. And that was still not working. So what the communists did is absolutely unheard of. They put food stamps on food. These were not food stamps like here in the U.S. where you can get free food. These were only permits to buy food. Please be patient – I will explain more about these hard times later. The communists knew that people like my father were always capable of making money somehow, or maybe trading for services. They wanted to break them down. They wanted to nationalize the whole country. And it took years. I remember that my father was struggling and struggling.

In 1950, the communists did something horrible that showed again what kind of creeps they were. Stealing all the big businesses was not enough for them. Breaking down the owners of small businesses was not enough either. They were finding out that many people had saved cash for their retirement or for a rainy day. Since checking accounts didn't exist, people had this cash under their pillows or in shoeboxes. The communists also couldn't stand imagining that somebody would have more than they had. So they made a decision and announced that from this point (in 1950), the existing money could not be accepted because new money had been printed. If someone wanted to exchange old money for new, they were welcome to do so, but it would be in the ratio of 1 to 5. This meant that you brought five old krons to the bank and they gave you one new one in exchange. However, it would work only to exchange up to 10,000 krons. Anything above 10,000 would result in an exchange rate of 1 to 50! Fifty old krons gave you one new kron! They also announced that all exchanging must be completed in one week! Since this "wonderful" news hit everybody by surprise, it created tremendous chaos. Huge lines of people were going into the banks with a lot of "old" cash and after doing their exchange, leaving with "new" cash that was next to nothing. What a rip-off! And the communists, again, very proudly, called this "the national exchange." Of course, the new money was printed with propaganda pictures showing happy workers and farmers as well as a lot of decorations using Russian red stars, hammers and sickles. This was completely disgusting!

Then came the time when they started to harass our family. The secret police came in the middle of the night and they were searching for something illegal, such as literature against communism – or searching for weapons – or searching for some printing machine that would be used for printing some literature against the regime. They knew, they knew really well, that they would not find anything like this in a tailor's home. But the reason for this was to harass – to scare my parents and also to show in the neighborhood that we did something wrong and we must be bad people. Since my father refused to join the Communist Party, they wanted our family to be the black sheep in the eyes of some of our gullible neighbors. At that time, some neighbors had already joined the party, pretending they believed in it, but really joining to get the benefits.

There was not much difference between the secret police (KGB) and Gestapo. They were torturing people and we knew that. Everybody knew that, but there were people who didn't care. They still joined the communists.

They said, "OK, I will get benefits out of it. I will get the membership pin and I will get the power. I'm going to be a crook, but it will pay off." They were power-hungry and most of them were not educated people and were not really good people in the first place. They had the same mentality as some people during the Hitler era who joined the Nazis. Communists had a way of convincing people by teaching children in the school how wonderful the world was going to be under communism. I will say more on this later. Now I have to get back to the harassing because it will be hard to get back to it later.

The communists tried to convince people to join them. First, they tried convincing us peacefully. They were lying and promising all sorts of wonderful things. But most of the people didn't believe them, so these lies were not working. So they started harassing people. This was taking place in the middle of the night. They arrived with sirens and emergency lights and woke up the whole neighborhood. They wore dark brown long leather jackets. They were very noisy and they were threatening. I remember being a little boy, standing against the wall by the bed, crying, because they were making this huge mess. I was somewhere between three and five years old. Because my father was such a craftsman, capable of working on any type of fabric as well as leather, he had a huge collection of supplies – snaps, hooks and eyes, needles, thread, buttons, etc. He had them well organized in separate drawers and boxes. These creeps came and mixed everything together on the floor and just walked in it. They yelled at my parents, "We didn't find it this time, but we will be back." They had guns but, thank God, they didn't use them. The whole thing was very scary. Everyone knew that the Stastnys were the guys that were being investigated and that was their goal. But even this didn't work.

So, then they started to put food stamps on the food. But these food stamps, as I mentioned earlier, are not the same food stamps that you have in the United States. Here in the U.S., if you qualify, you use food stamps as money to go to the store and buy food against the value of the stamps. But back then, in Czechoslovakia, food stamps were totally different. It was only a PERMIT to buy food. You still needed money to pay full price for the food. But if you didn't have those food stamps, the store couldn't sell you the food. The grocer had a certain amount of food, and he had to report that he sold the food for a certain amount of stamps. He had a large reporting sheet of paper where he recorded the item sold and glued the food stamp to that spot. At the end of the day this sheet had to be turned in to the officials.

The amount of money collected had to balance with the amount of stamps collected. Food stamps were given to everyone, but in differing amounts. If you were a member of the party, you could get many more. My mother would go to the store with plenty of money, but when she got home, she was crying because she didn't have enough stamps to get what she needed for our family. This was another method the communists used to break the back and spirit of the small businessman who refused to give up – my father and people like him! The lady who ran the store was from the neighborhood, and my mother had known her for years. But she couldn't sell the food to Mother because Mother didn't have these food stamps. So, the only way for Mom to get the food was to go and beg in the neighborhood from door to door and ask some old ladies who did not have use for all of their stamps.

A neighbor might have food stamps for a month for five liters of milk, but she only needed two liters. She gave my mother stamps for three liters of milk. My mother was collecting – and some ladies even came on their own because they felt sorry for us. It was not easy for them either. Communists also put these stamps on other everyday needs – like soap, fabric, shoes, etc. We were totally stuck. We couldn't buy anything. Luckily my father was a tailor, and my mother knew how to sew and knit also. She knew how to make underwear, blouses, and shirts. So we were well-dressed. I remember that I was always getting shoes and clothes after my brother because he was older. I also remember my mother was making a couple of sweaters for us for Christmas one time. She couldn't go to the store and get yarn. Instead she was getting it from a factory that was making some kind of sweaters or sweatshirts. She was able to get some leftover material after they finished cutting fronts, backs and sleeves from the big panels. They were throwing these little corners in the garbage. My mother picked up a big bag of them. For a number of evenings, she was just separating the yarn from these leftovers and tying it together. It was so colorful like some decorative fabric that you see in Mexico. She made two sweaters, and she was doing that after her everyday work late in the evening. When she was done, she gave them to us for Christmas. I remember that just like today… The sweater had a design like the head of a rabbit with the big ears. It was a row of black rabbits, a row of red rabbits, rows of blue, yellow, purple, pink, etc. She made cuffs on the sleeves and also on the waist. And as we were growing, she was making the cuffs longer and longer and longer. I ended up with a disproportionate sweater with cuffs more noticeable than the whole design.

My father's choice not to join the Communist Party was because of his integrity, honesty and pride. And it was also just doing the right thing. Joining was the wrong thing to do. You couldn't just go with the flow and ignore the facts of what the communists were doing. To explain it to you: Father started and worked on a prosperous tailoring business and then some uneducated idiot who had just been given power, came to tell him what to do. Furthermore, innocent people, wrongly accused and publicly prosecuted, were in jail. Some were even executed. During WWII, many Czech citizens were trained in England as fighter pilots, paratroopers, and resistance fighters. These patriotic people had fought against the Nazis and had saved many lives. But since these people had been trained in England and had seen what kind of dirty politics were coming from Russia, the communists didn't give them any mercy when they returned to Czechoslovakia after the war. They deserved to be recognized as heroes and instead were persecuted by the communists. Some of them were executed and many others ended up in very nasty political labor camps that were worse than the German concentration camps. Many of them died there.

History was twisted and rewritten. The communists wanted us to salute the Soviet Union for every little thing that they did and would do. And we knew that everything in Russia and coming from Russia was very primitive and nothing but lies and propaganda. The Russians didn't have any sophisticated or advanced factories or industry of any kind. They needed us to help them and help them big time. They were like leeches. They couldn't figure out or develop anything on their own. The only thing they were able to do on their own was to copy somebody else's product and they couldn't even do a good job on that. They took somebody else's product apart and then copied it, actually I should say, they TRIED to copy that but they always screwed it up. They didn't have the skills to produce anything right. It was in everything. Watches, cameras, radios, tools, cars, airplanes... And then they put their name on it. And then they were bragging about "their" products and achievements. On the radio and in the newspapers they were always shouting to the whole world about their superiority. In the movie theater before any movie was played, there was 15 minutes of their "news propaganda." It was so obvious and cheap that every honest person hated it. The communists wanted us to applaud and be thankful to them for this, in my opinion, robbery. It was just awful!

I'm not saying that my father was hanging on the truth that we were also liberated by the Americans. This was just one of the pieces of the puzzle. Any honest people couldn't bring themselves to join the party. Try to imagine yourself in this position. I will try to give you an example. Let's say that you are a CPA and have your own accounting business, but it doesn't require inventory or real estate. Your business is mostly in your head, in a file, and in your briefcase. There were many people who were attached to the land, attached to their properties, machinery, something they created, their buildings... Your accounting business might not be physically large, but its value is the same as somebody's warehouse and you are attached to your business. Somebody is coming from some country like Japan, China, Mexico or Argentina, coming here to take over and tell you that your business is now their business and you will have to speak their language. You have to listen to and sing their anthems. You have to look at and salute their flag all the time. To join them, you have to lower yourself to their level, to their dishonest group of liars, thieves and losers, and pretend that you like it.

This is what happened to us. Every classroom in our country had large pictures of the communist presidents of Czechoslovakia and Russia as well as a picture of Lenin placed next to the blackboard. These pictures were also found throughout the whole country in every official building and public place. I saw more Russian flags in my childhood than our own Czech flags. We were listening to their Russian anthem, watching their movies, being required to speak their language, dancing their native dances. And they were telling us all the time how beautiful it is, how "well off and happy" we are under their leadership. They were messing up the factories. They didn't know how to make cars. They didn't know how to grow corn. They didn't know anything about anything. Pollution was incredibly bad. Their currency was so bad and didn't have any value in the world market. The police were hiring crooks to have power, and these crooks were being well paid to spy on us and report us to the regime. One of the most horrible things was that there were some people who were looking at the situation and greedily and dishonestly thinking to themselves, "Well, we don't like this, but I am just going to join the Communist Party to get them off my back and have some benefits out of it." That is really selling yourself and your country and betraying your fellow citizens.

Whoever joined the Communist Party was not a friend. It was quite dangerous to discuss anything with somebody that you knew was questionable. We discussed our feelings with only the closest friends – someone you knew would not turn you in. You couldn't say to a communist, "I'm not going to join you because you are a crook." It was very dangerous. You would have ended up in jail. Your negative answer had to be put into very clever, careful and diplomatic words. But in the back of your mind you would be thinking, "Get off my back, you SOB!"

4

Teen Years and Learning a Trade

I wanted to be an artist. My dream was to be a photographer or a cameraman making movies. After graduating from high school, I wanted to attend some art or photography school, but the doors of every art school had been closed for me because the corruption was very, very bad. I cannot say that I was an excellent student, not at all, but I believed that I had talent for the area

Louie's high school graduation picture

that I wanted to pursue. Art motivated *When I was 16, with my brother's guitar.* and excited me. I spent a lot of my time doing it and enjoying it. Since I was a young boy, I always enjoyed going into art galleries. Of course, I played soccer and other games with the kids on the block, but art galleries, and especially photography studios and shows, were very special for me. I felt frustrated that the communists wouldn't give me the chance and opportunity to attend any art school where I could express myself. The students in these schools were children of prominent people or of big movie stars or well-known singers. All these students and those who wanted to be in these art schools had connections to someone in the industry. I didn't stand a chance since my father was only a tailor, and he was not a communist either. Of course, members of the Communist Party who were paying big bucks under the table had priority.

Every time I applied to a school like that – and later on when I tried for a job to be a cameraman or an assistant, or any job working for filmmaking companies – they always welcomed me first before they realized I didn't fit their corruption mold. I always knocked on the door, walked into the office, and asked for the boss by name. He would say, "Oh, please, come on in and sit down." He was impressed with my pictures and portfolio, and his next question was, "Who sent you?" And I was stuck right there. I couldn't make up some stories with some lies, and I didn't have money to pay him under the table either. And he would say, "You have very nice pictures, and I wish you luck." And that was it. Place after place after place. I was trying so hard to get my foot in the door of the film business.

Later I ended up in a photo lab developing film for amateurs, like the

Picture taken at age 16. Panorama of Wenceslas Square in Prague at night – a five-minute exposure.

one-hour photo labs we have here. But it was a job that was really low paying and didn't offer any creative opportunities. On my own I would do creative photography such as night scenes of the city, landscapes, playing with light and shadows, pictures of everyday life in the city. To make extra money I would take pictures of wedding ceremonies at the courthouse. Those weddings under communism were not as fancy as those you see today in the U.S. The ceremonies were quite simple, almost done assembly-line fashion, not giving photographers much opportunity to be creative. But it was extra money for me.

Everyday I was showing my boss at the photo lab new pictures that I was taking in my spare time. We discussed the photos, what was right, what was wrong. He really liked my work and we talked about photography with a great deal of excitement.

I was young (17 years old), and one day, this guy was looking at me and saying, "George, why are you here in this lab?" I responded, "When I was hired here I was told that if I worked here for five years, I would be given

the materials to take and possibly pass the test so I can be a cameraman – or a professional photographer." He took me on the side and said, "George, I have to tell you something that I shouldn't be telling you. I'm putting my neck on the line. Do not trust these people who promised you that. They were promising the same thing to those two girls over there. One has been here for seven years and the other one for thirteen years and they didn't get anywhere. They're still here. You are also going to be here and working for minimum wage. This is the closest you are going to get to photography." I felt really lousy and disappointed. I didn't have any freedom, any creativity in this job. And he said, "You are going to go into the military like all young men, and you might get married while you are there. You might come home to a family that you will not be able to support on minimum wage. There is no future here for you. If I were you, I would just run from here as fast as I could." It was a very depressing moment for me... I was so down. I was walking as if I didn't have a soul. I just kept walking and was close to crying. I wasn't even thinking straight. I kept wondering, "What has happened to my dreams?"

I got together with a group of friends that I saw on a daily basis. They were visiting, talking, joking, and I was not saying anything. I was so down. One of them said, "George, what is wrong with you?" So I told them. Two of them, Louie and Mirek, who were in an electronics trade school, got excited and said, "George, one guy in our class just quit and there is an opening in our school. The timing is incredible! Take it. You are good with tools and mechanics. Come on. You can take this school with us." It was just like Carolyn and my old friend Maggie always said, "When God closes a door somewhere, He opens another one somewhere else." So I grabbed this opportunity. It was a two-year college sponsored by the large electronic factory, Tesla, and it actually turned out to be a very good experience for me. I learned quite a bit about mechanics, electricity and electronics. We were taught how to use sophisticated technology such as oscilloscopes and electronic testing meters as well as mechanical equipment such as lathes, mills, grinders, etc. After one year the school administrator came to me and said, "George, you have been selected as the second best student for college. So, we are going to be sponsoring you. Here is the application for college."

I couldn't believe it! My dream was going to come true! I was in seventh heaven! Great! "Art School!" I thought immediately. I am going to be an artist after all. I filled out the application and turned it in. The administrator came yelling and screaming with his hands above his head, saying, "George, are you crazy? You requested 'Art School.' We want you to be an electrical engineer and work in our factory. We don't want you to be an artist. You must be an engineer." I said, "I don't want to be an engineer. I am just here because I can't be an artist. I have always wanted to be an artist." He said, "George, you are going to be an engineer – just change it." He added, "I will give you 24 hours to change it." I said, "I don't need 24 hours. I am not changing anything." He said, "If you don't change it, you will not go to college, and we will give this opportunity to the next best student." And I said, "Oh, well." And that was it.

5

A Huge Explosion!

W hen I was 17 years old, I experienced something on January 16, 1962, that I will never forget, and I would like to share this with you. First I need to mention a few facts to put you into the picture. As you know by now, we were living in a very large, seven-story building with 56 apartment units located next to a very busy intersection in Prague. I would estimate there were from 150-200 residents living there. Our apartment home was on the sixth floor. Louie's family lived behind their former pastry shop (that the communists had confiscated) on the street level. This building was well built before communism from bricks with very thick walls with a large basement with lockers where residents stored various items that weren't often needed. Like sleds, winter skis, bicycles, etc. But the most important purpose for

Building where we lived since I was born. Taken about 1960.

these lockers was to store heating fuel – coal – as well as some firewood. In the center of this building was a five-person elevator that ran in the middle of a large granite spiral stairway.

That day, in the afternoon, my mom sent me to the basement to get two buckets of coal. While loading the coal, I smelled natural gas. There were a couple of other people in the basement at that time and all of us were complaining and concerned about a possible gas leakage. We reported our concerns to the building custodian. He told us that he had already reported the smell of gas to the gas company a week ago. They had sent a technician to check it out. He had briefly checked things and reported that everything was fine and we had nothing to worry about. The custodian promised that he would report the smell again.

Perhaps you are wondering why we used coal for heating when the building was plumbed for natural gas. Well, at that time, most of the people, us included, used natural gas only for cooking because it was convenient and fast. However, it was very expensive to use. Since coal cost less, we used that for heating in freestanding stoves. Our family had one gas stove and oven for cooking and two coal heating stoves.

After my trip to the basement to get the coal, I needed to finish my daily chores. Then I left for the rest of the day, spending time with my gymnastics buddy at the gym. I came home around 10 PM, sat down in the kitchen and tried to get a late evening snack. Mom was also in the kitchen and my brother was just approaching from the hallway, when IT happened. The biggest, loudest, longest ear-splitting **BANG** that I have ever heard and experienced! All our doors were forced open by violent air pressure, breaking the locks and hinges. All windows totally blew out. My brother braced himself in the doorjamb and held on for dear life. Everything that was lightweight like curtains, newspapers, tablecloths, etc. flew out of the shattered windows. The whole building shook as if there were a huge earthquake. After the last pieces of glass landed noisily on the ground outside, there were a couple of seconds of absolute silence followed by horrifying screaming coming from outside from people who had been hurt by flying glass and other debris. My brother and I looked out our shattered window and saw an unbelievable mess throughout the entire intersection as well as the bus terminal directly across the street from our building. We saw piles of bricks, broken furniture, and bedding mixed with merchandise from all the stores that occupied the ground floor…

At that point we had no idea what had happened. Our instant thoughts were that some large plane had crashed into our building. Or maybe that a passing fuel tanker truck had exploded. A few seconds later I remembered the natural gas leakage. My brother and I told our mom to stay put and we went to investigate and figure out how to get out of the building. As we were going down from the sixth floor, we were witnessing bigger and bigger damage. With each passing floor, we saw not just missing doors but also cracked walls, then broken walls. When we got between the second and third floors, the walls were completely missing, as was the stairway. The elevator was completely shattered into toothpicks and buried in the rubble. It was horrible to see. Our friends' apartment with their photography studio was totally missing. There was absolutely nothing left, just a huge ugly opening. We had no doubt that they all must have died. These were horrifying moments with a lot of screaming and panic. Of course, the power was out and it was late in the evening, so we were completely in the dark. Mysteriously, there was light outside, probably from automobile headlights. Looking outside from the dark through the dust and rubble was a scene I will never forget. Some rescue workers, probably volunteers, were already working to free trapped people. They were yelling at us not to come any closer or lower because the stairway was gone. My brother and I were looking at this shocking scene and then at about the same time, we both thought that our father could have been in the elevator at the time of the explosion. We knew he would be coming home from seeing his friend in a nearby neighborhood and he really could have been in the most devastated part of the building. It was a very scary thought, but we really couldn't do much of anything about it at that moment. We could only hope that this wasn't the case, but we couldn't stop worrying about that.

We needed to go back to take care of our mother, and we made a plan not to mention our worry about our father. When we got back up to the sixth floor, Mom was calm but still in shock. We started to prepare ourselves for our departure from the building. We didn't know if the whole building would collapse, but we knew we wouldn't come back any time soon or maybe not at all. Since this was in January in the middle of a very cold winter, we were putting on warmer clothes. In the middle of all this, Mom suddenly stopped and said, "Gosh boys, where do you think our father is?" At that moment my knees were giving up on me. I felt like I was coming apart emotionally and physically, but I knew that I must stay strong and pacify and support my mother. I tell you, it wasn't easy, but I think that I managed.

Getting out of the building wasn't as bad for us young boys, but it was very difficult for older people. We weren't helping only our mom, but all others who needed help as well. We made some very funky ladders with a lot of help from outside volunteers. It took us at least 45 minutes before we were finally able to get out onto the street. By then there were dozens of emergency vehicles and rescue workers helping people and searching for victims. The police were blocking the whole area for security reasons, not letting anyone in who didn't have a reason for being there. Even though this disaster happened at night, there were immediately thousands of lookers around the area.

My brother and I were searching for our father and while doing that, I ran into my friend Louie. We were very happy to see each other. It was a miracle to see him alive because their apartment was very close to the epicenter of the explosion. We were both searching for our fathers and promised that we would notify each other when we found them. Louie was very poorly dressed in only long johns and plastic raingear that he got from some stranger who happened to be passing by. Louie was also barefoot which was pretty bad since we were walking on a layer of sharp debris and tons of broken glass. Then I spotted my father talking to my mom – I was so happy and relieved that I was rushing through the crowd to hug him and when I finally reached him, his reaction was typically "parent." He didn't know how much we had worried about him and the first words that came out of his mouth were, "George, how many times do I have to tell you that you must wear a hat on your head when it's so cold!" Oh well, typical parent! I think it's kind of funny under the circumstances. But the most important thing was that our family was happily reunited.

Louie was not as lucky. His father was found in the basement with both legs broken. He had fallen into that big hole in an attempt to rescue his family. Many people were seriously injured, many with permanent consequences. A number of people lost their lives. Physical and emotional damages as well as sacrifices were huge. Material losses were astronomical.

This entire disaster could have been prevented if one person, the government-run gas company employee, would have done the job correctly and responsibly and hadn't had the typical socialistic-communist work ethic attitude of "I don't care!"

The first night after the explosion we were able to stay in the homes of friends and neighbors. For the following ten days we were stashed in various hotels, and then we were moved into new but unfinished apartment buildings in three different locations in Prague. Luckily, Louie's family and my family ended up in the same building again.

6

Military Service

In Czechoslovakia, every young man, 19 years old, must serve two years in the military, Army or Air Force. You don't have a choice or option not to join. It's part of your life, normal and mandatory. I was assigned to the Air Force. Louie went to the Army. It was really the very first time we were separated. Since we were born, we were living in the same building and in our 14 years of education, in the same classroom.

When you are being recruited, besides checking your physical health, you are also assigned to a certain MOS (military occupation specialty). Since I was a graduate of electronics school, I asked if I could be a mechanic or a repairman for electronic equipment. The recruiter was looking at me with an expression, "What do you mean?" I wanted him to understand, so I explained, "I mean to be somebody who knows how to fix military radios. Like a radio mechanic." He replied, "O.K.," and he made a note of that. But when I was actually drafted, I realized that I was assigned to be a radio operator, which was a big difference. Radio operators were soldiers who communicated using Morse code from one military radio station to another. This could be from base to base, or from ground to air, or even from a moving vehicle. All this communication was in Morse code and also in secret codes that made this broadcasting complete gibberish and prevented "the enemy" from breaking the code and understanding the message. The key to break the code was changed daily. I thought at first, that I would be able to be a radio operator, but very quickly I realized that this would cause a big problem and affect my mental health. When I was in training, the officers were forcing us to send and receive so many letters per minute, and it was seriously messing up my brain. I just couldn't speed up, and I really, really honestly tried. I was in emotional trouble. I want to be sure you understand that I wasn't trying to get away from being in the military. I didn't have any problem being in boot camp. I could put up with all that physical and mental training, along with a lot of harassment, just fine. I think that I really enjoyed the military lifestyle (being proper, keeping my things clean and in order, a lot of physical exercising, etc.).

I explained to the training officers and my higher commander that I couldn't be a radio operator. They ignored me and as a result, I started to stutter. I went to the military doctor who sent me to the main military hospital in Prague for an evaluation. When I returned to the base with the paperwork, the evaluation stated that I couldn't be a radio operator because my superior officer would be responsible for my health. The captain was looking at these papers with his supply officer, asking the question, "What are we going to do with soldier Stastny? He has to stay with us but we don't have a job for him." So they sent me to a neighboring barracks to the woodshop and my job there was to simply keep a wood stove burning! A couple of days later, when I was getting ready to leave my company to go to the woodshop, the supply officer (who was a high ranking warrant officer) stopped me and he said, "Hey, I was looking at your background and your education and I think that I can use you as my assistant. You are going to be doing a lot of writing for me and keeping track of inventory."

And that is exactly what happened. He taught me well about this job, and I learned a lot. I gradually stopped stuttering. Not even a year later, this supply officer applied for a higher position at a different location and was accepted. He became a finance officer at a different air base. I think that I lucked out because I was immediately promoted to his position. It was a perfect solution for everybody. I became a very important "supply officer" with a very low rank.

I was in the Czechoslovakian Air Force for two years. The communists had an interest to recruit as many members as possible to the party. When I was in the second year of my service, they started to ask me and tried to recruit me. If I had signed up, I would have been promoted immediately to a higher rank. They came to me a number of times and asked. I could not say, "Go to hell!" My name would have been mud. So, I would say, "You guys, I am really honored. I think that I have to discuss this with my family. This is a very serious step." As a result of that, I got leave for two or three days to go home, something that was very difficult to get since leaves were reserved for soldiers as a reward.

Now I need to explain to you the difference between being in the armed forces in Czechoslovakia and in the United States. In the military in the United States, you get paid even if you are the lowest ranking soldier. Your work is from maybe 7:00 in the morning until 5:00 in the evening. After that, you can put your uniform in the closet, put on civilian clothes and go anywhere you want if you don't have duty that night. You can do any sports, any hobbies, chase girls, take them dancing or for dinner. You can drink, work on something, or do absolutely nothing. It's up to you. You can do whatever you please. The next morning you have to be back in your unit and in uniform. In the Czechoslovakian military, you were in uniform at all times. You don't have any leave and you are in a barracks for two years. They give you leave as a reward but you have to ask for it. If you want to go to the movie off post, you have to apply for it and it must be signed by your officer. He will say, "Stastny did well," or "Stastny didn't do well," and he will let you go or not. To be able to go see your parents, your family and friends in your hometown, was a big reward. Every soldier in the communist army or air force had a right to go on vacation for ten days every year. Otherwise you could leave for one or two days only, as a reward.

So I was granted leave time to discuss joining the Communist Party with my family. I came home, and my parents were happy to see me and after welcoming me, they asked, "Why were you able to come? What is the reason?" And I answered with a grin on my face, "I have to discuss something 'very important' with you – I have the opportunity to be a member of the Communist Party." They rolled their eyes and gave me smiles back and I knew the answer. They knew that I knew the answer also. We didn't have to talk about that any further, and I enjoyed my two days with my family and friends. When I came back to the barracks, the communists asked me, "Are you going to join us and be a member of the party?" I replied, "Well, I discussed this responsibly for a long time with my parents, and they indicated to me that this is a very large and important step. And we think that I am not ready yet. I would not be doing a good job for you. Let me get a little bit older and more mature."

Many people wonder at what age someone could make an independent decision to join the Communist Party. The lowest age was something like 19 or 20. The communists had a political program for all ages. I've already mentioned the "Sparks" and the "Pioneers." The next step was the Union of Communist Youth. They were older teenagers (9th graders to 18-year-olds) with blue shirts for their uniforms that were worn for special occasions such as May Day celebrations. When these older kids were acting as leaders for the younger Pioneers, they also wore their uniforms. It would be just like here with the Boy Scouts and their leaders.

The communists had to lure young people with something attractive. These groups were going on trips, playing games, competing, but the whole idea behind all of this was political brainwashing. The highest step of this systematic brainwashing was to be a full-fledged member of the Communist Party. At this point, you were given a Communist Party pin. You paid some dues to the party, and the benefits started coming. We had one cousin who joined the Communist Party, and he distanced himself from the family because of that. Even though we grew up together as cousins and saw each other frequently, we never really wanted to have anything to do with him anymore. He was the son of our favorite uncle, Charles. But when he grew up and joined the party, we were just like, "Whatever, whatever…" He was trying to justify what he had done. He said, "Well, I have a family. I have to support a family so I had to join." And we were looking at him and saying, "Well, we don't have a family? Stop with your excuses. We don't buy it."

Back to my military career. Because I was a supply "officer," I was gradually promoted to sergeant. I should have been a warrant officer, but because of my background, not being a party member, I couldn't get any farther than sergeant. Under communism it works this way… You have your credit – not financial credit. But your credibility, your history, goes with you. Because everything is run by government, all companies, schools, military, everything is under one government. So it goes with you. They didn't have computers back then, but they had files. My file was following me from place to place. There was no way you would go somewhere and they wouldn't have a file on you. You couldn't have access to your file, but the government would have it.

After two years working with these officers, we kind of loosened up and could talk about things more openly and personally. I still saluted, but it was not as strict anymore because I was close to leaving the military. Close to the end of my service, two high-ranking officers were telling me over a glass of beer, "George, when you came to the military, your file was full of red flags. You were described as a very dangerous person. Not someone who would go along with the communists or with anybody. A rebel. Very dangerous." They were looking at me and saying, "George, you are a great guy. You should have been a warrant officer a long time ago." Actually, I had gone to school to be a warrant officer. I was one of the best students and passed all sections of the test with flying colors. I was the only one out of 60 who was not promoted because I was not a communist. There was no way I could be promoted because everyone from warrant officer up HAD to be a party member.

There was another guy, who was a sergeant like me, and because he had a college degree and was in an important position, they wanted to promote him to the officer rank – to be a first lieutenant. And they couldn't because he didn't want to join the party. I remember the situation with this guy. He was very close to his time to go back to civilian life after almost two years in the military. I can still hear it just like today... A captain who was directly responsible for promotions was telling this sergeant, "You really are hurting yourself. You are going to go to the civilian world and the retired reserves as a sergeant, not as a lieutenant." And this guy said sarcastically, "I can hardly wait..." I was very surprised when I heard this, because this kind of sarcastic remark would have nailed this sergeant. Maybe he had some kind of high-powered guardian angel watching over him?

I need to explain something important to you, but please don't take it as bragging. I think I was able to zigzag through the system and get the best out of it because I was popular which started in high school. I was playing guitar from an early age, and I knew many popular songs, something that our generation really liked. Many of my high school friends loved to sing, as did I, so they liked me and I liked them!

Playing guitar with many high school classmates enjoying singing.

I enjoyed so many sports and hobbies. One of my favorite sports was gymnastics, and I was a member of one of the top teams in the district. My biggest hobby was photography. I was developing pictures for other kids. Back then photography was nothing like today with digital and "point and shoot" cameras. At that time, you wouldn't be able to take any pictures without knowing what shutter speed was and how it worked, what the f-stop and depth of field was, the size and speed of the film, etc. I was one of very few people who had his own good camera with a professional flash along with a dark room and all the developing equipment. I worked hard every summer to be able to purchase these things. I was showing some of my own pictures to some teachers who thought highly of me because I was ahead of many kids when it came to art and handiwork. If something needed to be fixed in school, the teacher would ask who could fix it; the whole class would say, "George!" Later on, when I was in trade school, thanks to my older brother, I already knew how to use many of the tools that we were learning about.

I was popular in the military, too. I started my own business – selling cigarettes and candy after hours. Soldiers were in uniform for two years, 24 hours a day, even sleeping in military pajamas. But after hours, when most of the officers left the post, the barracks were still full of soldiers. A couple of hours after dinner, people started to feel like eating again. Candy bars, chocolates, soda pops, beer (drinking age in Czechoslovakia was 18 years and still is). I was going to the local store (a good three mile hike from the barracks) and carrying things back to the post in my backpack, selling each item for 20 cents more. Doing business was like a hobby for me. Even officers were buying cigarettes from me. So, I made some connections with these officers – remember, you had to be a communist to be an officer. Because I was living under this communist system, I had to talk to these people. I might reject my communist cousin, but I couldn't reject a superior officer in the military, who might be very close to me in age. I might be playing soccer with him after hours but I had to respect him as a superior officer. Sometimes we would be playing music and these guys would come and listen. We could not say, "Go away." We had to put up with this. It was a part of the life there.

When I was a sergeant in the supply area, I was running supply for food, clothes, bedding, furniture, ammunition, weapons, and all kinds of equipment – in millions of krons (which today would be almost millions of dollars). My position was very important and it also came with quite a bit of power. My company commander, the captain who I was working under, needed me. He was demanding that I be very accurate with the inventory. He needed me to perform well. On the other hand, he was trying to make me happy so he was giving me slack on some other things. When I needed to go and play music with my Dixieland band, or when I asked for some time off, he cooperated with me. I was too young to understand these things at first, but later on I started to see what was behind this cooperation. He started to talk about this cooperation also. When it came to inventory, we were both responsible for it, but he was the one who would get into bigger trouble if there had been mistakes. He made real sure that I understood all the laws, and all the math that was behind it, and also all of the tricks – lots of tricks. If you are in charge of so many vehicles, equipment, material, furniture, clothes, food, weapons, ammunition, coming and going, inventory always changing on a daily basis – there was always a chance of problems developing. There were always situations where on the one hand, I was short of some material that has been lost, stolen or miscalculated and on the other hand I had too much of something else. I had to shuffle and trade under the table with supply officers from other divisions so inspectors would never find anything wrong. So the captain made very, very sure I understood all these things that were illegal but were important to do to come out clean for everybody.

Myself in uniform, playing music everywhere we could – this time at the river.

I remember that I wanted to tell you something else, so here is another good story from my military experience. I was about two months away from finishing my service. We felt like we owned the place. I was playing in a Dixieland band that we created with a bunch of soldiers there. I played guitar, and I also had made a banjo out of a broken drum and a broken guitar. It was kind of a "guitar" banjo. It had six-strings but the sound was not that good. It was in tune, but it was like playing on a coffee can. It looked like a banjo! Later I bought a real tenor banjo when I met a man at a national military competition who played tenor banjo.

I had an office with quite a bit of space with a small warehouse behind. There was an upright piano in the barracks (military property) and we moved it into this warehouse. After hours we always pushed the piano into the office since it was a bigger space. We would jam in the evening for hours. There was also a huge safe in the office made of strong steel and five feet tall. I would sit on top of the safe, playing my banjo or guitar with the group. In the evening just the younger officers – the newcomers – would be around. They were those guys that would be on duty for the night in the barracks to overlook everything and keep things in order. We were not scared of them. We didn't have the rank, but we had some experience and some seniority.

Playing music in the city on the bridge, on the street… people always stopped to listen… we loved it!

One time I was walking to dinner and as the supply officer, I should have been the one that made sure all the soldiers were marching in precise formation, being properly dressed as they marched to dinner or anywhere else. I should have been a proper example for them. But I said, "To heck with that. That's just for new soldiers and for appearance. I'm hungry, so let's go for dinner." I wasn't dressed properly myself! Instead of putting on my shiny boots, I had on my old holey slippers. I didn't have on a hat as was required at all times by military law when outside. I might have had one behind my belt, but I didn't have it on. I didn't have my uniform jacket on either. My shirt was unbuttoned. On one shoulder, I had the insignia of a sergeant, but on the other shoulder, I didn't have anything. It was missing. I was walking with one of my friends, who was a lower rank than me. I had a spoon sticking out of my pocket. I looked terrible, just like a hobo.

We were walking on this big military airport – 3,500 people – like a city in the woods behind the barbed wire and towers. We were walking on this main drag (a long street) to dinner when I suddenly spotted somebody in the distance in front of me. He looked very different. I kept looking at this person without saying anything. But then as he got close enough and I could see better, I saw all the stars on his shoulders and medals on his chest. I couldn't believe my eyes. I said to my friend, "Hey, look! Do you see what I see? Is that someone from a movie? Who or what is this guy?" I was pretty certain he was some sort of general that I had never seen before. I knew everyone on the whole airport having lived at the air base for two years. I was familiar with all of the high-ranking people. I knew this guy did not belong here and I said, "This guy must run the whole Warsaw Pact. He must be some hotshot general, maybe all the way from Moscow. A really, really big rank." So here we are. It was too late to avoid him. I couldn't salute because I didn't have on a hat. In the American military, you could salute without a hat. But in the Czech military you had to have on a hat. So, I had to salute somehow, but if I didn't have a hat, I still had to give him respect – by looking at him with a still, sideways glance over my shoulder, and I started to march at attention. My friend and I started marching like military robots. But I was in slippers! I looked terrible, absolutely terrible! He stopped us and he stopped us in the strict military way. You always addressed the person by the rank. But in the communist military you always start to address people, "Comrade." That is the first word that must come out of your mouth. Comrade General, Comrade Captain, Comrade Sergeant, Comrade Major, or whatever. So this guy said in a very strict military voice, "Comrade sergeant, or whoever you are (because one shoulder insignia was missing). Come here."

I marched up to him in my slippers. And I reported myself to him, "Comrade General, Sergeant Stastny…" He started to talk to me strictly, and he said something that totally scared me. He said, "I have made an unannounced visit to your facility here – to see for myself how things are in this airport after hours. And here you are, walking and looking like a bum! You are going to report yourself to your Supply Officer tonight, and I am going to come to your barracks for an inspection tonight. What is the number of your company?" I was dying and my butt was tight. I knew that the Supply Officer was the guy who should take care of everybody to be sure nobody would look like this. And ironically, it was actually me! I was scared to death that I would end up in the jail. And then I would have to serve another year or so.

The idea of dinner was over immediately. My friend and I started running back to the barracks. I called everybody together, told them what happened to me, and that this hotshot was coming to inspect our barracks tonight. I only hoped that I would look different enough that he would not recognize me. We started scrubbing – cleaning, polishing, and making everything look beautiful and shiny. And after all this exhausting work, we were waiting and waiting for him. But he didn't come, and he didn't come, and he didn't come. My friends said, "Hey, he is not going to come, forget him. Let's go on with our business." They meant our business of playing music. So, we pulled the piano out of the warehouse, into the Supply Office. We opened beer and started to play our Dixieland. Another great party! When we were in the middle of the fourth song, the door opened and through the cigarette smoke, which was so thick we could barely see each other... I saw this person. I saw those shiny stars, that shiny hat. And here I was – the highest-ranking person again. I jumped down off the safe. I was probably back in my old slippers by then and I was, again, barely in uniform. When I landed, I called everybody to attention. And I started to report to this general – how many people are present, what we were doing, etc. But he stopped me in the middle of my sentence. He said, "I like that music. Go on. Go on, guys. This is my type of music. Just go on." So we started playing again, but very carefully. And he said, "No, I mean like you were playing before. Just get into it." So, we cut loose. And after a couple of songs he said. "Sounds good. Looks good. Nothing wrong here." And he left. I never found out who he was. Luckily, the music saved us...

Several paragraphs ago, I was saying that I don't want to brag, but now I want to brag! I was brought up by parents who taught me how to work, how to achieve my goals, how to be persistent, and how to be productive. From my early teens, they couldn't buy me things I wanted like bicycles, cameras, etc. They never gave me any money because they couldn't. I never asked for it nor did I expect anything. It's like the saying, "If you are hungry, I won't give you a fish, but I will teach you how to fish so you can take care of yourself." I would say, my parents taught me how to fish very well. The reason for talking about this now is because I've just spent a lot of time talking about me being in the military. When I was recruited and leaving home to go to the military, saying good-bye to my parents, my mother gave me three krons and a sandwich. She told me, "Take good care of yourself and good luck." Two years later, when I was leaving the military, I came home with my own car, an old one, but it was a car. It was very unusual for someone my age (21) to have his own car in 1965. I also returned with a guitar, banjo, amplifier and many other little things as well as a small savings. I hope that you understand I was proud of myself. For my entire life I have been a productive person. I've worked hard and never regretted that. I enjoy looking back and seeing the results of this hard work.

7

Factory Work and Marriage

I came home from the military, and I started to work again in the same factory (Tesla) where I had been trained, with my friends, to make televisions, radios, and telephones. This factory was a large company with many branches throughout the country. In Prague alone were three branches. Where I worked had 1,800 employees. I had an interview with one of the bosses. At the interview, he asked about my experience. I told him about my work in the military with a lot responsibility for a large inventory. He immediately knew where he wanted me to be. I became the supply manager for one big department, but not an administrator, because I was not a member of the party. My main responsibility was to be sure the work in our department was going along smoothly and productively. If any problem came up – broken equipment or tools, mistakes in or missing schematics, defective or missing parts – my job was to solve the problem immediately. I believe that I was pretty good doing the work that I was assigned to, but my heart was not there. The job paid only a little bit more than some others I could have chosen. Of course, I could have had a lot better job, with a lot better pay, if I had joined the party. Here in the United States if you are not doing well, if you are not motivated, if you don't have the drive, if you don't

My first car – Czech-made Aero, 1938.

have the skill, you will be working for minimum wage and scraping the bottom. But if you are motivated, have drive, are a go-getter, have a dream and a goal, and you go for your goal, then you are very likely to be successful.

You have much more than the minimum wage and there is no limit how high you can go. All of this is up to your ambition. That is the difference. Under communism, you could have the drive and motivation and everything – and you might have only twice as much as the minimum wage. But the bottom line of my point is, in the United States, the difference between those who have the drive and those who don't is so much bigger.

The title of this chapter sounds like I got married in the factory, or at least I found somebody in the factory that I married. No, that's not the case. When I got back from the military, it was like a reunion with some of my old friends, of course, including Louie. None of us had any serious relationship with a girl and we all liked to go on Sunday afternoons to dance. It was very popular in Prague, dancing in the big dance halls and concert halls with live, big band orchestras. We called these dance gatherings "tea dances." I don't know why, because nobody was drinking tea. They didn't even serve tea there, but it must have been some old tradition, so we just kept calling these gatherings "tea dances." And that's where I met Helena. She was there with her younger sister Zdena. One of my friends, Mirek, started to dance with Zdena and I danced with Helena. We danced together most of the afternoon that day, and we started to date. Helena lived on the northern outskirts of Prague. She worked in a nearby factory in the machine shop on a lathe. She was the girl that I liked because she was very friendly to my friends and she fit right in with our interests of hiking, biking, camping, swimming, skating, volleyball... She was never whining about being tired, cold, or bored. She was very athletic, and when she was a teenager, she was on a league handball team.

We were not dating for very long, just about four months, when Helena shocked me. One day when I came to meet her in front of her work, she said, "George, I am going to get married." I was shocked. I had no idea that she was engaged to someone else. I felt hurt but I tried to keep my cool, so I asked, "Who is the lucky man?" And she shocked me again when she answered, "That lucky man is YOU!" When I recovered, I asked her, "Please, can you explain a bit more about this?" And she did. Helena and her sister had promised each other a long time ago that when they got married, they would get married together. Well, Zdena was getting married and asked Helena to get married also as they had planned. So Helena agreed and since I was in the picture at that time, we went along with the plan. And that's how we got married. Shortly after our wedding, Helena started to work at the same electronics factory as me and we were commuting together. And now

I can go back to my job in the factory.

Because I was responsible for a lot of people's work, I had access to a lot of things. Let's say that some guy was working on something and he didn't have the right blueprint. I had to go into the archives to find the correct one. But they had only the original and they couldn't give me that. So, I had to go to the printing department to get a copy. But back then, it was much more complicated, not sophisticated like today. Those blueprints were humongous. You might have a television blueprint, or one section of the TV, or some electronic equipment that is testing TVs, or a phone – these blueprints could cover an entire workbench and were very complicated. So, in the meantime, somebody's tools might not be working right. And I had to fix them myself or find someone to fix the tools. It was an interesting job – a very demanding job. I was all over the factory – all over the place. Very soon, many people knew me and I knew them.

There was this guy who was the factory Communist Party committee member. He was always yakking at these communist meetings. He saw me flying around the factory – running up and down on the stairways trying to beat the elevator, zigzagging among the people, and he started to notice me. Of course he noticed me – he wasn't doing much, just wandering through the factory and smoking. He recommended me as a good potential member of the Communist Party. He was telling everybody that I am fast, so full of energy, that I would fit right in…and I thought, "Here we go again!"

But now, because this entire story is just like a puzzle, everything is connected to something else that I haven't mentioned yet. In Prague under communism, there was a lack of housing. It was especially hard for people with families. There was no place for them to live so they were staying with parents. But this was not working very well. I guess I don't have to explain why. Everybody needed their privacy and couldn't have it with this type of living arrangement. So to have your own place, your own apartment that you rent, was a very important thing but very difficult to get. Communism was not working very well, and construction was not working fast enough. For what they were paying us, nobody was working very hard. Apartment buildings were the property of the government including those that the communists had stolen from private owners. We had to apply to the government to get an apartment. When I got married, we applied for an apartment and they told me that I would be on a waiting list. I said, "OK, when am I going to get an apartment?" I was not expecting what they told me. They told me I had to wait 13 years! And even that was "maybe." Because of this corruption, somebody who paid under the table or somebody who became a member of the Communist Party jumped over us on this waiting list. So, we would always be on a waiting list for 13 years.

But there were some priorities. If I would join certain work forces that were being heavily promoted, like coal miners, military, police, or construction, you could speed up the process. Of course, if you would join the Communist Party, you would also jump over others. So, this communist committee member in the factory approached me and told me that if I would be a communist, I could get an apartment faster. I came up with the same story that I would have to think about it. He approached me again, and my response was that I didn't have enough time to think about it. Finally when there was no way to avoid it, I had to tell him that I was not ready and that I was not right for it. I kind of hurt his feelings, but I didn't mean to. I was very polite, but I just didn't want to be a communist. This is an important moment for my story about how I escaped from Czechoslovakia, because one part of the story will come back to this guy. He was a big shot communist – in both the factory and in the neighborhood. Later he was getting back at me and it was like getting revenge. He started many times trying to buy me or lure me saying, "George, you could have skipped six years on the apartment waiting list." He was offering to arrange a wait of seven years instead of thirteen years. I didn't take it. In my mind I was thinking, "You can have it." It was at this point when a new thought was born in my mind – "If I can't get an apartment from the government, I will build something myself and I will do even better. I will build my own HOUSE!"

I started to be very unhappy in the electronics factory. I was dreaming about doing something else, something outdoors. I almost felt claustrophobic inside the walls of this factory and I feared this would be the case for the rest of my life. I just wanted to do something that I was proud of. For instance, planting a tree, fixing a road, or something else where I would see results that would be more obvious at least to me and hopefully to others also. Working in the electronics factory, I felt like I was getting nowhere – I was just a tiny piece in the whole machinery. I had no living space. I was married and I needed a nest for my future family. I couldn't get it anywhere, so I was even more convinced that I would build something myself. Of course, I was not expecting any freebees and knew that I needed to take care of myself. But I needed to be able to do so. I would never make enough money in the factory – nobody made enough money under communism to be able to honestly purchase materials and build a house. You always had to do something fishy. So, I said, "OK, if I work in the electronics factory, it is not even going to give me the skills to build a house." A new idea began to form – I thought about working for a construction company. This would give me the opportunity to work outside. I didn't mind working in rain or cold conditions. I am an outdoor person and being trapped inside the electronics factory was bothering me more and more. Besides, in construction, I could learn some very important skills that I would need for building my own house.

But to quit working in the electronics factory was not very easy. They had the right to keep me there – to make me work there – for at least a year. In some cases, it was three years. But there was a way around this if I would go to work for one of those needed jobs that I mentioned earlier – coal mining, agriculture, construction, military – then I could leave immediately. So, it was time to go forward with my plan to work for a construction company, maybe driving a big truck, or operating a big crane. But I didn't have a commercial driver's license. Getting that license was very expensive and time-consuming.

Quitting my job at the factory was interesting and difficult because of those stupid laws. It showed on my work performance that I had lost interest in working there. I was not doing my job right and I did not want to be there. My boss talked with me about it. He said, "George, you have to change your attitude. Your mind is somewhere else. We need you to work at the speed that you used to do." I told him I was not interested in making a career out of this job. He was a big communist and he was one of those who almost believed in it. He took me aside and tried to talk to me like a father. In this conversation he got a little bit too personal and after he finished, I was tired of hearing him and I just said, "OK." He didn't change any of my thinking. This conversation didn't do any good. And now a little story of a stupid young man – me.

Right after this conversation with the boss, I went to the supply room just to rest and wander. There was an older lady, Maria, working behind the counter. I had a good relationship with her, one of constant teasing and laughing. In this supply room were rows of shelves full of material and spare parts to which I had access because of my position. On the end of one row was a metal closet that I opened. And there was a rope – like you use to make a lasso. I said to myself, "Hmm, since Maria's not here at this moment, I will surprise her and hopefully scare her. I am going to pretend I am going to hang myself. And when she walks in, she will totally freak out. I will scare her…" So I took this rope, made a loop, put it on my neck. and was looking up to see where I could pretend to hang myself – a place where I could also support myself with my arms. While I was looking with the rope around my neck, something really, really weird happened. Unknown to me, in the next row of shelves was my boss, who had been giving me this lecture just a couple of minutes ago. He saw me, but I didn't see him. He thought he had gone too far, and he was just rushing to stop me from hanging myself. He hugged me and said, "George, please don't do this. I didn't mean to be so hard on you!" I just looked at him with wide eyes thinking, "I just wanted to scare Maria." And he kept saying, "George, please don't do this to yourself…" He obviously cared about me. It was nice on his part and silly on mine. He wanted me to stay and work there. Now, my idea of making a joke and scaring Maria had backfired on me.

The next day I apologized to him and politely explained that I really want to work somewhere else. I was thinking to myself, "You can make me come and be here, but you cannot make me work. If you won't let me go, I will come and I will just not work." This standoff lasted only one day and after one day, I was called to the personnel office. They said they could hold me there one year by law. I argued that if I would work in agriculture or construction, they would have to let me go immediately. I took the first construction job that was available to me. Unfortunately, it was a very bad and low-paying job working on a road project using a shovel and pick, working in a group of non-educated gypsies. I felt as if I were on a chain gang, but it was a good experience. I knew that this was just the beginning of going after my goal of building a house.

Before we could begin, we needed to find and purchase a parcel of land. We actually lucked out because there was a parcel available within walking distance from where we temporarily lived in the attic of Helena's grandparents' house. When I say temporarily, we knew this would be for a few years. We were able to buy this piece of land for a fairly reasonable price. Because it was a small, triangular-shaped lot, at the end of the town, and not really considered easily buildable, it was less expensive. It was cheap because of the difficulties locating a site for the well, the septic, even the house itself and all the while staying away from the required distances from the property lines. There was no city water, sewer or even electricity. It took a lot of planning for me to figure out how to do all this, but in the end, I was successful. I was very happy that I could finally start to build our "nest." I dedicated almost all my thoughts to this happy project. I knew that it would take a long time and a lot of hard work but I had a vision that at the end, we will have our own beautiful house on our own property. We didn't have children yet, but I was already dreaming about how happy we would all be there.

8

Warsaw Pact Invasion of 1968

After we bought the land, I started to collect building materials when suddenly, all our excitement was interrupted by the horrible events that struck on August 21, 1968 at 3:00 AM. Czechoslovakia was invaded by its own allies and our lives changed forever. Nobody who lived through that time will ever forget the terrible memory of that historic day!!! But first, let me give you some background of what led up to this attack.

The Czech people wanted to get rid of communism in 1968, and they wanted to do it peacefully. But the Russians didn't want to let it go. It was at the end of the 20-year contract between Russia and Czechoslovakia. The contract had been signed in 1948, and now it was 1968. The contract was running out, and the people were saying, "We don't want to sign another contract with those leeches." It was a very exciting and hopeful time. The spring of 1968 became a very important time in Czech history. People felt that freedom was coming and was almost here. People started to discuss political issues more openly, even in all the media – TV, radio, newspapers. Everyone began to talk freely. Oh, it was such an exciting time! People even began speaking out against communism and communists. Politicians started turning around and playing a different tune. The situation was turning around very rapidly. We had a new president, Ludwig Svoboda, and a new head of the Communist Party, Alexander Dubcek. They were on the people's side.

By the way, many Czech names have a meaning to them, such as my name "Stastny" which means "happy." "Svoboda," the president's name, meant "freedom!" What a clever coincidence! Ludwig Svoboda was a highly decorated Czech army general who was a WWI veteran and also fought the Germans in WWII. He had led some important battles, fighting side by side with the Russians against the Germans. Of course, at that time nobody had anything against the Russians. They were protecting themselves from Hitler just like everyone else, including Americans. The Russians were pushing the Germans from the east out of Russia back to Germany through Czechoslovakia and liberating our country at the same time. The Americans fought the Germans from the west, and as I mentioned earlier, they liberated Czechoslovakia as far as Pilsen where they were ordered to stop. The decision was made to allow our "Russian brothers" to liberate the majority of our country. However, at that time, no one was aware of the dirty politics of the Russian dictator and commander Stalin who had already made plans to overtake all of Czechoslovakia.

But, back to Ludwig Svoboda. In WWII, he was actually fighting on the side of the Russian Red Army. He was being promoted as a big hero. He was a hero, no question about that. But in order for him to be a "communist" hero, he needed to also be a communist! He joined the party. Over the next 23 years, from the end of the war through the era of the communist totalitarian regime, Russians promoted him more and more. They were putting him higher and higher on a pedestal and in March, 1968, he became the Czech president. However, the Russians didn't realize or believe that he still had some integrity, and in the spring of 1968, Svoboda was protecting the interests of the Czech citizens. He began supporting and promoting the citizens' excitement and hope of getting rid of the old communist regime and starting a new free era.

Alexander Dubcek came from a different political background. He was Slovak by nationality, younger with a college degree from a communist political school. He became Svoboda's highest government partner as the head of the Communist Party. Both men were showing their patriotism and true dedication to all the Czech and Slovak people and quickly became very popular. Everybody liked them. They were members of the Communist Party, but they took an entirely different approach to government and politics. It was spring of 1968, and the new era was starting! We called this era "socialism with a human face." This was, however, something that the communist leaders in Moscow couldn't put up with. The Russian president, Leonid Brezhnev, warned the new Czech leaders a number of times to stop this new way and return to strict communism, or he would do it himself. People's excitement was so high that nobody believed that we would be turned back to dark times. But Brezhnev showed us his nasty teeth. He was a real pig. I was not the only one who hated him. The whole country did.

Brezhnev made a sneaky plan against Czechoslovakia in 1968. He ordered military maneuvers of the whole Warsaw Pact, but the Czech military was not part of this. They were not included. I better explain who were the members of the Warsaw Pact. Of course the largest member and biggest player was the Soviet Union (Russia). They surrounded themselves with a number of their little satellite countries. These countries were a lot more advanced and sophisticated than Russia. They included Czechoslovakia, Poland, East Germany, Hungary, and Bulgaria. By the way, for the younger generation, the Warsaw Pact was created to show the West that we could protect ourselves against NATO (North Atlantic Treaty Organization) that was mostly led by the U.S.A. But I honestly believe that the U.S. never had any problem with Czechs, Hungarians, Poles, or Bulgarians. The creation of the Warsaw Pact was all politics because of Russia.

Now back to these Warsaw Pact maneuvers. They were taking place in Poland. The Czech military was kept out of it and we really didn't pay any attention to any of this because we were so gullible and felt that freedom was coming. As we found out later, the maneuvers were only an excuse and part of the horrible Brezhnev plan to storm the peaceful people of Czechoslovakia and start his dirty occupation of us.

Russians kept coming! Unfortunately I have only these few pictures from my brother. Communist censors seized my own pictures showing the huge magnitude of the invasion when Simon tried to mail them to me in the U.S.

The invasion of our country came on August 21, 1968, 3:00 AM. Hundreds of thousands of Russians and Warsaw Pact soldiers stormed Czechoslovakia all at once. Military power that you cannot imagine. Planes, tanks, armored vehicles, trucks, everything. Nobody expected anything like that. Anything like that at all. The magnitude was overwhelming. We were stunned, very angry, sad. Many people cried. It was hard to believe and we couldn't conceive that the Russians actually arrested the highest members of our government, including the chairman of the Communist Party, Alexander Dubcek. They flew all of these men immediately to Moscow, held them there for a week under incredible pressure and threatened them that they must stop the new era of freedom and democracy. Our president, Ludwig Svoboda, flew to Moscow two days after the invasion, trying to help stop this plan of treason by Brezhnev. It was a horrible trick by people who were claiming that they were our brothers and trumpeting to the whole world how NICE communists are.

Our whole nation came together and became united against the Russians. At that time, even communist military officers in Czechoslovakia started to fight back. They couldn't fight back by shooting – that would have created a real massacre – so they were fighting any way they could. Incidentally, later I talked to two captains who I served with, who were later kicked out of the Air Force for being part of the military resistance at the air base during the invasion. It was very obvious to me that they didn't regret being kicked out under these circumstances. They told me that the airport where we had served had been one of the points for Russian planes to land early in the morning of August 21. When the Czech Air Force officers found out that the Russians wanted to land on our base, they immediately – there was very little time because of the surprise attack – put all of the trucks and other heavy equipment on the runways so there was no way that Russian planes could land. Nevertheless, the Russians landed at the international airport in Prague as well as many other air bases and civilian airports all around the country. They landed wherever they could. Since Czechoslovakia is in the middle of Europe, the military forces of the Warsaw Pact crossed our borders from all directions of the neighboring communist countries. Huge numbers of them kept coming by air and by land. They were instantly everywhere, taking over key points – government buildings, banks, etc.

One huge key point was the radio station in Prague. A tremendous fight broke out between the Russian military and ordinary Czech civilians, with the Czechs trying to barricade the radio station with anything they could

Russian tanks in Wenceslas Square, 1968, taking over key points. Peaceful citizens surround them, trying to explain to Russian soldiers that they are in the wrong place and should go home.

find – buses, any construction excavating equipment, cobblestones pulled from the streets – to create barriers.

These Czechs didn't have any weapons, but they had shovels and picks that they used to poke holes in the fuel tanks of the Russian vehicles, setting them on fire. I saw many burning tanks on the streets. The Russian military power was so great that they broke through our barricades anyway. I saw city buses used for the barricade flattened by the Russian tanks just like a soda can on the street that was run over by a car. However, the barricades had slowed them down and had given the radio technicians a chance to go underground and continue broadcasting from a secret location. The regular news anchors continued their broadcasts, which is important to know because we could recognize their voices. The Russians, along with some Czech traitors from the old conservative Communist Party who didn't want to break away from Russia, quickly established a new radio station where they were broadcasting their lies and propaganda. Our original radio station kept us informed about what was happening and very strictly advised us to be calm. They did not want us to provoke the Warsaw Pact forces, to give them any excuse to fire on us. It was so difficult because we had already taken to the streets and

Above and below: Invasion of 1968 – next day, smoke settling after the fight for the radio station.

No comment!

You could see results of Russian soldiers' driving skills throughout the country.

absolutely hated the invaders! The Russians were already shooting at us in some places, killing many people and injuring many others. Most of these casualties were in front of the radio station. It was just plain murder. They broke the law and all the rules of human rights with absolutely no regard for our national sovereignty. They attacked us; they were the predators and we were the prey.

Our radio station also gave us advice on how to fight back. One bit of advice was to confuse these foreign forces by taking down all the street signs and information and directional signs on the highways. So at night I got my wrenches and took down the signs in our area. Some nuts and bolts holding these signs in place were too tight or rusty so I couldn't take them off. Instead, I bent them like you would close a book so no one could read them. This was our way of fighting back. It was so interesting to see that in one night, all the road and street signs in the entire country disappeared. The Russians were lost. They didn't know where they were and their maps were useless.

It was a very difficult time. We were trying to resist peacefully. I need to remind you that the Russian language was a required subject to be taught at all levels of school in Czechoslovakia. This actually backfired on the Russians during this time in our history because we could communicate with their soldiers. We were trying to convince them they were in the wrong place. We tried to talk to them peacefully, but we were also angry and with raised fists, we were telling them, "Pack up and go home where you came from! We never asked you to be here in the first place!" We were making large signs in both languages, Czech and Russian, everywhere we could. And we were very specific what we thought about them! I will give you a few examples:

- Head Up – Never Hands! (In other words, keep your pride and never surrender)

- We were taught to fear the West – now we are attacked from the East!

- Not a drop of water or a crumb of bread to the occupiers

- Russian soldier! What will you tell your children when they ask you why you were in Czechoslovakia?

- Russian export = tanks, lead, death!

- Yesterday, Brother. Today, Murderer!

- Truth is greater than power!

- We don't want Russian-style freedom!

- Moscow is your city – Prague is ours!

- An agreement by force doesn't count! (We used this slogan after our leaders were forced to sign an agreement that we would go back to the old style of communism.)

- Brezhnev = Hitler!

And absolutely everywhere, in many languages including English, "GO HOME!"

We had a hard time reading the faces of Russian soldiers, what they were thinking, and when we talked to them, they didn't know where they were and why, but most of them really didn't care. Some of them thought that they were in Greece. The soldiers were hungry, exhausted, dirty, and

We made Russian signs everywhere. This streetcar carries the sign "OCCUPIERS, GO HOME!"

many of them didn't appear to us to be educated people. However, some were obviously educated and we could communicate with them quite well. There was one case that I know about, of one Russian soldier who committed suicide. When he found out what was really going on, he just took his own life. It was too bad that the person who was dead was not Brezhnev since he was the guilty one.

It was interesting to see how the different nationalities (Hungarians, Poles, East Germans, Bulgarians) of the Warsaw Pact reacted. All of them except the Russians, when they realized where they were and what was going on, left immediately. And we never saw them again. In my opinion Brezhnev

Absolutely nonsensical destruction at the National Museum by Russians – all windows broken, most of the exhibits inside destroyed, irreparable bullet holes in the stone building. No one could understand why. Russian sign in the toilet seat says, "GO!"

didn't mind that they left. I think that he wouldn't have been able to trust them to go along with his dirty politics anyway.

A week after their arrest, our president and members of our government returned to Czechoslovakia. They provided us with a very difficult and emotional speech on the radio. They said, "In the name of peace, and to save our nation, we had to sign a document that our country will go on in the spirit of communism." The whole country was listening and we knew immediately that our hope for freedom was gone. It was horrible news but we really couldn't do anything about it because we were surrounded everywhere with hundreds of thousands of Russian soldiers ready to take over by massacring us. We had to face the reality that even when we had to go back to the "dark ages of communism," we would have to go on with our lives and get the best out of it. Just the same old story and lifestyle that we hated and knew so well. What a terrible betrayal!

Russian soldiers took over a number of our key military bases, moved in and established themselves there. Gradually, the officers brought their wives and kids and created their own military communities. The wives of these Russian officers were the very lowest class of people that I have ever seen. They had absolutely no manners but they had very demanding behavior everywhere we saw them. They always stood out from the crowd everywhere they showed up. They were cutting lines in the stores, demanding special attention, demanding that other people speak their language, being obnoxious, noisy, just awful. We were forced to live with all of that Russian invasion, and I hope that you can understand how much we hated them, and we still do. The sharp edge of this hate is not there anymore, but I don't think that we will ever trust them, and I don't think that we should. They should be ashamed of themselves.

.

9

What to Do?

Now I need to mention an important event that created a huge dilemma in my mind – what to do about my future. Through these events of the invasion, the borders between the Eastern Block were literally opened, allowing invading troops to enter our country. There was so much chaos everywhere, that even border crossings through the Iron Curtain to the West were not guarded. This opening allowed many Czechs who could see what was coming, to sneak out to freedom. The Russians allowed the borders to be open for a very short time, just a couple of days. In my opinion, they did this to get rid of the rebels, people who might cause trouble later. They let them go. Then they really sealed the borders and put their boot on us hard. They started with a really strict and hard regime.

My father had had a similar opportunity in 1948. He had planned to escape after he had such a hard time with the communists trying to take over his business. His plan was to escape with the whole family. He had made arrangements with a smuggler who was working and living in the area of the border between Czechoslovakia and Austria. My father had already met with the smuggler, paid him, and made arrangements that we were going to go through the swampy area, a place where there were fewer border guards. The Russians felt they didn't need to guard this area as heavily because of the danger of being in the swamp. Many people who were trying to escape drowned there. My dad knew that there were some positive cases where people were successfully smuggled through the border. But Father's plan collapsed when my mother backed off at the last minute. My father wanted to do this, even with our dog, to start a new life in Austria or maybe Switzerland later on, or maybe in Canada. I was very small, only four years old. My mother was very gullible and sheltered and couldn't see what kind of era was coming. She just couldn't handle it. She broke down and started to cry, and my father couldn't leave without her. So the whole plan collapsed at the last minute. I never knew about this as a child. Father told me about this when

I was an adult.

So now back to 1968. I had the same opportunity. I wanted to leave. I was the one who initiated the thought, but unfortunately, at the same time, I had already started to build the house. I didn't want to back off from my dream of building it. But on the other hand, I saw this opportunity to get out of there. I went to my parents and talked to them about it. My parents at this time were too old to go through this escape. My father saw the opportunity that he didn't take 20 years earlier and he encouraged me to go. But my mother said, "Don't do it, George. Stay where you are." I still asked my father if he had any contacts or connections of any kind on the other side of the Iron Curtain. Somebody to give us a little bit of help or advice of where to go and how to start our new life in a new but strange country to us with language being one of the biggest problems and obstacles. That's my experience. Try to put yourself in an immigrant's shoes. I will give you a little idea of what it's like.

You are in a new country with a different language that you can't speak. You need a job and you don't know how to ask for it. You can't even ask for directions because you can't read the signs. Any time when you want to read something, you feel as if you are blind. When you want to say something, you feel mute. And when people talk to you, you feel like you are deaf. That's why first contacts for immigrants are an important help. My father did give me some names, but these contacts were too old. They were 20 years old. In 20 years, a lot of things changed. People changed addresses, phone numbers, and they also died. I wanted to involve my brother and his wife. I didn't want to go without them. They were looking at me like I didn't think things through enough. My brother is made out of a different mold than me, and he thought that it would be a very wrong step. Helena and I were young and I wanted to leave, but not alone. At the same time, my back-up plan or excuse was to build our house. After all, we thought we would be able to live a fairly peaceful life in Czechoslovakia even under these harsh circumstances, so we knowingly missed this opportunity and we stayed put.

I also want to explain that the biggest reason that kept me staying and going on under communism was our relationship with many good friends including my brother. Music, hobbies and sports that we enjoyed together were so much fun. That was the fuel for me to be happy and exist.

From left: my brother, myself and Simon having a good time.

10

1969: Marking the First Anniversary of the Invasion

The first part of 1968 was very promising, but the second half was very nasty. 1969 was very difficult. The communist regime became very strong and strict again. The communists focused on the white-collar people of the working class. They started to investigate every single manager, foreman, and boss of every company through the whole country. They created thousands of "investigative" committees and called on the carpet each boss, manager or leader one by one and one at a time. These people were interviewed about what their personal attitudes and beliefs were concerning the Communist Party and the regime. Also, what did they think and remember about 1968. The communists didn't like the outcome of August 21, 1968, and wanted this event to be totally forgotten like it never happened. It was very typical of the communists to change history and the facts in their favor. These investigative committees also demanded that the bosses sign a positive statement about the Communist Party. It was done this way because the communists wanted to scare people and they knew it was very difficult to say anything against the regime when you are on the spot just by yourself. It's easy to demonstrate against something when you are one of a million doing this, but when you are put on the spot by yourself, it is very hard. If you say anything against them, the consequences would be at least losing your job. You would be on the "No-no list" which would also be tragic for your family. Most of the people got scared, swallowed the bitterness, and signed that they believed in communism. It was harder for some than others. But all of them felt ashamed. Although an overwhelming percentage signed this statement, there were still many people who didn't sign. They just couldn't and they ended up with a feeling of pride but paying a very high price. I met some of these people time to time and you could tell that they were former leaders and bosses. I saw them having to do the worst jobs that you can imagine; for example, shoveling very dusty low-grade coal into a hopper at the heating plant. And for the lowest pay possible.

The entire country, the whole working class felt betrayed because of these investigations. We were very sad and upset. The communists knew they had everyone under control and that everyone liked or must like them. They felt they were on the top again. We wanted to protest but we couldn't. That would have been against the law and punishable. From the spring of 1968, from all the hope that freedom was coming, to the spring of 1969 was a huge difference in the overall mood of all the people. You could tell it on their faces. Nobody could express themselves in public. People were living a kind of gray life under suppression and disappointment with no sparks, color, happiness or excitement. We could have fun and talk openly only in private circles where we were sure that we knew everybody well.

Singing with Simon for Standa's birthday at the Ski House.

And then someone started with a clever idea of how to protest peacefully and demonstrate that we don't agree with the communists. Somebody started to spread the news that on August 21, 1969, the first anniversary of the Soviet occupation, anybody who disagrees with the regime will not use any public transportation and will not do any shopping that day. This news spread through the whole country faster than airmail! I need to say and remind you of two important things. Personal computers didn't exist in 1969, neither did email or cell phones. That was one thing, and the other thing was that in Czechoslovakia, especially at that time, very few people were using their cars or motorcycles for commuting to work. Almost everyone was using public transportation for commuting. Well, guess what? The whole country was walking that day! Nobody was using public transportation. Buses and street cars were running absolutely empty. The whole nation was walking and no one did any shopping. The stores were empty. It was a very clever and peaceful way to show that no one agreed with communism! The police couldn't do anything about it! I would like to say that my wife and I walked a really long distance to work – 11 miles one-way. Since our work started at 6 AM, we started to walk at 2 AM and we were very happy to do this. The sidewalks in Prague were very crowded, but people were very disciplined and polite to each other. It was such a beautiful experience. This protest was not repeated again. I guess it wasn't needed because the communists already knew how we felt about them. They stopped being so cocky in the newspapers, radio and TV, at least for a while.

11

Building a House

I had a very good friend, Vasek Suda, who was ten years older than me. We were distantly related on Helena's side of the family. Vasek was a truck driver for a big construction company where I would eventually become a driver as well. He had two sons, Vasek, Jr. and Bo. Back then, Bo was just a boy, maybe eight years old, Vasek, Jr. was two years older, and I was twenty-two. Both boys were very nice kids. Bo had an interest in photography, and he wanted to take and develop pictures like I was doing. He got involved in this hobby pretty heavily and his father, Vasek, was supporting him 100%. Vasek, Jr. started to play guitar and wanted me to teach him. I think I was probably their idol, and I felt very honored that these two nice boys wanted to be like me. As it worked out, I taught the boys how to play guitar and do photography, and Vasek in turn, taught me how to build a house. We were not horse traders but rather admired each other's skills, which worked really well, benefiting both sides of the friendship.

Vasek knew how unhappy I was in the electronics factory and I knew from him that I could make more money as a truck driver. He had told me earlier that whatever I wanted to do – work on a fixer-upper or build a house from scratch – he would teach me because he was a brick mason by trade.

When I started to work for the construction company, it was a big disappointment for my father. He always wanted me to be an architect or an artist. When I was a little kid he also wanted me to be a tailor, but it never happened. He taught me a lot about sewing. Learning how to sew was fine with me, but I never wanted to be a tailor. So, here I was working on the street with a shovel in dirty clothes and digging mud. When my father saw me working on the lowest level possible, he felt very bad, but I was happy. I was young and I knew that I had to do this awful work before I could get the required licenses for trucks, cranes, or big rigs. I took the job because I knew that I wouldn't do it forever. It was just one step I had to do. So I didn't really make a big deal about it. But my father was extremely unhappy, and he couldn't adjust to my way of thinking. He couldn't understand why I had a decent education and had a respected job in the electronics factory one minute and the next I'm on the street digging ditches! In the meantime I signed up for commercial driver's license classes. It cost quite a bit of money, but I got my license for big trucks. I started at the bottom, in the worst job for drivers – working in the city driving an old clunker dump truck. One year later, I was given a better vehicle and eventually I progressed to very good trucks.

Immediately I started thinking about building the house, pursuing my dream. As I mentioned earlier, we had this little parcel of land on the outskirts of Prague. The location was not the best, but it was what we could afford at that time and was close to where we lived. We were living in the attic of Helena's grandmother's house. It was one room that used to be for the storage of hay for Grandma's animals. We fixed the area so it was nice, clean and cozy and livable for the two of us.

I had a number of friends, but one particular friend was so eager to help me with my house project. His nickname was Simon. We had become very good friends years earlier. Simon was actually first my brother's friend and was seven years older than me and you will hear his name more often through my story. With Simon's support, I started immediately with my house building plans.

I need to explain to you that building a house in communist Czechoslovakia was a lot different than building a house in the United States. In the U.S., when someone says, "We're building a house," it means that they've opened the Yellow Pages or attended a home show to find an architect and contractor who will design and build the house for them. But many of these people don't even know what a hammer looks like and they still say, "We're building a house!" And I really don't mean to put them down. I guess it is a culture thing to say it this way.

Building a house in Czechoslovakia under communism was very difficult and very different from building here in the U.S. First of all, homes are built here out of 2x4's and sheetrock. In Europe they are built out of bricks or concrete blocks – also wood beams and steel beams. They are built to last centuries. Houses here might last centuries, but they really have to have a good roof. In Europe where the walls are made of bricks and concrete blocks, the structure can last for centuries even without a roof. So, I started to collect bricks. Bricks were expensive and that's why I collected old bricks from demolitions, making piles of them on our parcel of land. On Sundays we would go there and clean the mortar off the bricks with hammers.

Friends helping to clean bricks for future house.

I needed to have concrete blocks – just about 18" long, 12" wide and 9" tall. Those blocks were made out of a lightweight concrete mixture. They were also expensive, so I decided to make them myself. To make these blocks, I was using ash out of high-fire coal commercial furnaces located in various factories in the industrial part of Prague. The ash was like lava, very porous but very hard and light. We mixed the ash with sand and cement. The blocks were hollow to provide insulation for heat. I needed about 2,000 of these blocks for our house, and also 10,000 bricks, a lot of wood and many other materials.

It is important for you to understand that in communist Czechoslovakia, no building materials were available. Sometimes, clerks in building supply stores could be bribed to give you a few supplies, but for the most part, due to constant shortages, supplies were not available at all. It doesn't make any sense to me why these stores had titles like "Lumber Store" or "Building Supply" when there wasn't any lumber or building supplies in them! It would be like for you to go to a car lot to buy a car and there wouldn't be any cars there! Most of the time, there was no cement in the stores, something I needed immediately for making the concrete blocks as well as the rest of the house construction. If the clerk in the store found out that a shipment of cement was coming, you could bribe him under the table and he would send you directly to the cargo train. You would get cement right out of the railroad car. There would be a line of people who had paid under the table. So the cement never got into the store. The clerks in the store didn't even have to touch it. There was also a shortage of lumber. I'm telling you, people with this poor work ethic didn't produce much. Here, in the United States, you open any newspaper and there is always some sale at The Home Depot or Lowe's and many other building supply stores. They all are advertising and trying to lure you on some sort of special. They will even bring it to you for free if you buy from them. Here in the U.S., car lots are full of cars and sometimes, dealers will give you a free camera if you will take a car for a test drive. This is mind-boggling – in one society it works smoothly and beautifully, and in a communist society, it doesn't work at all. The bottom line is that under communism, it doesn't matter if you work hard or not. You get the same nothing for it. I really believe in free enterprise and the reward system.

Back to the reality of making my concrete blocks. I realized that since I knew that I would be making these blocks really by myself, I had to find out how to make them. I had to create some form, some kind of mold. I also had to have a hopper and a vibrator. I couldn't just go to the store and buy a hopper or a vibrator. Because no store sold them, I had to make them. I needed a welder to make them. But I didn't have a welder, so I had to make one. But to make a welder, I had to have some electricity. But I didn't have any electricity on the parcel. I had to bring the electricity from a block away.

Now we are getting into a situation in which communists lied to the entire world. They said they provided electricity to every house for free. So, here I was, wanting to build a house. I went to the electric company and asked for electricity. They let me know they couldn't help me. I realized I was on my own. So I asked them, "How can I do it – what are the requirements? What should I do?" They told me, "If you will do the installation yourself, we will come and inspect it for a fee and you can then have electricity, but we will not do the work or provide the material." So I was asking them all sorts of questions – what gauge the wires needed to be, how large should the poles be (I needed two of them), how to anchor the poles, how deep the poles have to be set, how big a concrete collar underground has to be used, etc. I felt lucky working for the construction company because there were many experts I could talk to. My big step from the electronics factory to construction started to pay off because of these contacts. In fact, when I started to work with a shovel, one of my jobs was digging these holes by hand for the electrical poles, so I had good experience. Today, no company would dig the holes by hand. Big equipment drills the holes. But back then, I had to do this completely by hand. I knew it was not going to be easy, but it could be done. I knew I had to cut the shovel short to have a short handle so I could fit myself and the shovel into the deep and narrow hole. If you have a big handle, you end up with a big hole. I learned quite a lot about digging! Building the house from scratch, especially with a basement, required a LOT of digging. Even now, when I am digging at my outdoor gallery or some other landscaping project, it is very useful. I don't want to sound like digging is my hobby, but I really like and admire people who are not afraid of a shovel!

So, I needed electricity. There was no type of store where you could go and buy what you needed, like the poles or electrical wiring, insulators, etc. You had to go and steal them from somewhere. Under communism your whole life is different. You always had to have money in your pocket to bribe and pay somebody off. You had to go and find a foreman or supervisor in some construction company who was pretending that those poles belonged to him when they really belonged to the government. This was 1969, and there was nothing in private hands.

By the way, at that time, even my father was working for the government where he ended up on the railroad. He couldn't handle the harassment, food stamps and high taxes anymore. He couldn't support his family with his disappearing tailoring business. He was labeled as a former businessman, and he had a terrible time finding any job. He refused to become a member of the Communist Party, and eventually he started as I did, with a shovel and pick, working at a very low-paying job on the railroad. He had a very hard life, but he never gave up. He is my hero. He had to learn a lot about totally new things to him, and considering his age, to me it's amazing what he had to do to support his family. It took years of hard work for him to progress from being a fine craftsman and tailor, to using a pick and shovel, to being a fireman on a steam locomotive, to finally being a second engineer on diesel and electric locomotives.

Now, back to my electricity dilemma. Here I was, trying to find the electric poles that I needed for my property. First, I had to find a lineman who worked with these poles and pay him under the table for something that didn't belong to him. Then he actually helped me load the poles onto the truck. I was also stealing the use of the company's truck and the fuel. I had to be prepared with some sort of lie or clever answer if a policeman or inspector were to stop me. There were police everywhere who had the right to stop me for no reason and ask, "Where are you going? Why are you not on the route you should be on?" I had this material on "my" truck that I "paid" for but with no receipt. It was this way with many other things.

I got the electric poles, and later also the wires, so I could start digging the holes. I anchored the poles 6½ feet into the ground with the anchoring concrete collars, one on the bottom of the deep hole and the other just beneath the surface – exactly as the electric company told me to do. I was climbing on these poles by myself, extending these wires, which carried 380 volts of electricity. I had to pull the wires into the box where the electric company would install the meter for temporary construction, just like if you were building a house here.

Since I had applied for this temporary electric meter, I went back to the electric company and told them, "What you told me to do, I have done. Please come inspect my work so I can get the meter and start to use electricity." They said, "We don't have time." Again, I said, "Please. I need to use the electricity." And they said, "We just told you we don't have time." That was their way of saying, "Pay me under the table and then we will have time." So I went out and got the equivalent of $100 into my hand and went back with the money in my palm. I stuck out my hand with the money in it, shook this same supervisor's hand, (he slyly pocketed the money) and said, "Hello, my name is George Stastny. I would like you to come out and legalize my electricity." And he said, "OK, no problem. I am going to send my guy out." So the guy who came out with the truck, meters, and seals said, "This is not legal. I cannot do this. We are not connecting electricity from wooden poles. The poles have to be concrete." I said, "Your boss told me to do it this way." And he said, "No, no. That was two months ago. Now we have changed the law. It has to be concrete." I tell you, you would kill somebody at this point. So, I gave him $50, and he said, "Well, I cannot do it. But I can kind of close one eye. I can do it if you will make a concrete beam that will hold and support that existing pole. It has to be 6½ feet underground and 6½ feet above the ground. You have to put two large bolts into your wooden post. And then you have to cut the post 18" above the ground – to be sure this pole will never rot. And the concrete has to have 18 rebars length-wise and done in a specific way." As a result, I had to make these concrete posts first (13 feet long), then dig two additional holes and cut through the existing underground concrete collars that I had just recently installed as instructed – a very difficult thing to do. I did all this and finally, the electrical company showed up for another under-the-table payoff and finally I had the temporary electricity.

So far I had made a welder and a form to make concrete blocks with a hopper and vibrator. Next I needed to test my equipment to see if I could make the blocks. Since I didn't have a mixer at that time, I mixed the concrete by hand on the ground. I made the first few blocks and it worked. Hooray! What joy! What a huge milestone!

But I knew I could not do all the mixing by hand. I had to have a concrete mixer, so I had to make one. It was another challenge. My friend Simon helped me to create this concrete mixer from an old oil barrel, a gearbox, and an electric motor. Simon was one of the most helpful friends, helping me a lot to create many things. Now that I had this concrete mixer, I could mix anything, not just light concrete for blocks but also stronger concrete for all other needs. Next I needed some platform on which to make the blocks. So, I made it out of concrete.

Every house needs water, so my next major and very important project was to dig a well. I dug it by hand with a pick and a short-handled shovel. Digging was a lot of hard work. The well was five feet in diameter and 40 feet deep. When I was inside the well and digging, my father always feared that the walls would collapse on me. At 34 feet deep, we finally hit water! The earth started to get moist, then muddy. Oh, we were so happy!

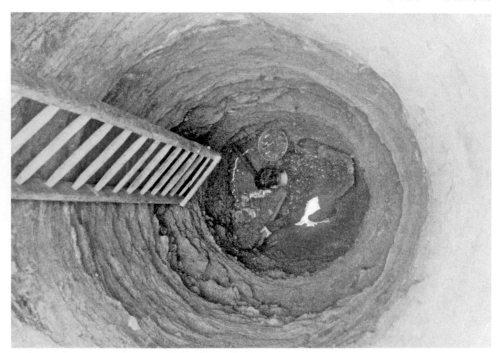

Digging the well. Look carefully on the right side and see me standing in the water, digging.

Finishing the digging became a little more difficult because of the presence of water. No one digging a well today can imagine what this is like. Today the drilling company comes with its machinery and no one has to be in the hole. We were using a primitive system for getting the material out of the well, just like in the old days – a round wooden cylinder, like a piece of a log, with a crank on its side, a rope, and a strong heavy bucket.

I had to make large concrete reinforcing rings that needed to be placed in the well to prevent the walls from collapsing. I started to make these rings before I actually began digging the well, and I kept making them through the process because I didn't know how deep the well would be, and therefore, how many rings I would need. These rings were four feet in diameter and two feet tall. I was glad that I had the mixer so I didn't have to mix the concrete for them by hand. However, I needed some kind of mold for making them. Again, I couldn't buy a mold anywhere, so I had to make it. I used thin aluminum sheet metal that I got through a friend, but it was too flimsy and since it was the only material available to me, I had to reinforce it. I did this with epoxy and fiberglass.

Making concrete rings for the hand-dug well. Helena's mother was always ready to help.

The reinforcing rings had to be smaller than the well diameter so they would fit freely inside. We filled the space between the rings and the well walls with sand. The last step to finish the well was to make a lid and install a hand pump. Later on, after the house was finished, I installed an electric submersible pump, but I kept the hand pump in case of emergency.

The whole process of making these huge concrete rings gave me valuable experience for my future business in the U.S. I learned quite a bit. In fact, I am using some of this same technique in making my planters and fountains. (The story will eventually give more details about my work as a sculptor.) The difference is the planters and fountains are pretty and the well rings were ugly!

It was a very exciting feeling!! We had our own little parcel of land with our own well and our own water! When I think back about this process, now I can appreciate how my father worried about me – having his son 40 feet underground with no reinforcing rings yet in place.

So far, everything I had to prepare and make, like the installation of electricity, making the welder, concrete mixer, form for concrete blocks and making 2,000 of them, digging the well, 21 large well rings, cleaning 10,000 used bricks – all that took me about two years. Considering that I had a full-time job and we could only work on the project evenings and weekends, I felt I was on schedule, and I was happy.

Finally, I started to build the actual house. I was planning on a very large basement that would have a shop, storage for coal, a coal furnace, a vegetable cellar, a food cellar, and a garage for a car. I cannot say I was hand-digging the whole basement. I asked the construction company that I worked for if I could use a couple of trucks, a backhoe and a couple of other pieces of equipment. I paid only for the fuel and the drivers' wages. We used two 5-ton trucks and dug out 20 loads of earth. But it was a very rough hole and I still had to do a lot of hand-digging, finishing the basement corners, digging the narrower trenches for the foundation, creating the sloping driveway to the underground garage, etc. It was roughly another 20 trucks of earth that was hand-dug and hauled away. Oh God, it was endless! Thinking back, a shovel was a tool that I used millions of times. I can't imagine that some people don't even have a shovel! Or some people have a shovel in the garage and the paint isn't even scratched!

My friend, Simon, was the one who helped the most with the construction. Vasek was also a big help. My ex-wife, Helena, was working very, very hard. Her mother was helping a lot. Her sister and my brother were helping quite a bit. As a percentage, I was there 100%. Simon helped me about 40% – especially in the beginning. And those other ones were maybe 10%. This was help on actual construction. After that, finishing the interior – electrical wiring, plumbing, woodwork finishing (I had to hand-make 17 doors from scratch) – all this was done by me alone.

There were shortages of building materials in general. For instance, there was no cement on the market. A number of times I had to pay under the table for supplies, and a number of times I was getting material from my work, but this was not really stealing. I will explain this to you. For instance, the streets of Prague were paved with cobblestones. Our company was digging these streets out for a number of reasons and replacing them with asphalt or concrete. For example, there might be an old water or natural gas line, or electricity under the street that needed to be serviced or replaced. After that, the company was not replacing those cobblestones. Most of the time they were sending someone like me with my dump truck to take the cobblestones to the dump. But instead of taking them to the dump, I took them to the house and used them as building material. I needed a lot of stone so this was a huge advantage. It was also very handy that I was driving a big truck at work. I wasn't really supposed to be bringing material to my house job site, but I did it anyway. I brought cobblestones, sand, whatever I couldn't fit into my car. When I dropped many loads of sand, the neighbors saw me and asked, "Could we have some sand, too?" It was difficult to say no. So I was providing a lot of materials for other people at the same time.

These actions were common "criminal" activity. You were stealing from the government because they stole from you in the first place. Everybody was stealing – everything and everywhere. The government was always telling us that everything belonged to the working class, so we simply took them at their word! Since everything belonged to us, we made a joke out of this and justified our actions with this slogan. "Since this belongs to me, I can take it and hope the police will not catch me!" The whole society was corrupted. Bribery and buying all sorts of things under the table was the way of every day life. There was no way that you would buy anything that was in high demand in any store without paying extra under the table. It was everywhere: in the auto parts stores, in the plumbing stores, in the lumber yards and building supply stores, and even sometimes in the food stores. My mother had to have a friend at the newspaper stand who would save her favorite paper, one with a little bit less communist propaganda in it. Can you imagine living in a society where you had to have connections in order to buy your favorite newspaper under the table?

Another area where you had to have good connections was the butcher shop. You couldn't buy good meat without having that connection. The shop always displayed in the window or on the counter big bones, lard, pigs' feet or something that was not desirable. The good meat was somewhere back in a locker. The butchers were selling the good meat only to people who would pay extra under the table – or to their friends who were providing some other services for them in return. I know that you might think that was a weird system. There was a network that you had to be part of or you would have a hard time to survive. You had to have your own butcher. If you did not have your own butcher, maybe you had your own plumber. You could get your meat through your plumber. It was complicated like this. The butcher needed somebody to fix his car. So the butcher might ask, "George, I have a broken transmission on my car and I need somebody to fix it." He is not telling you that for conversation. He wants or needs to trade services. You cannot say, "Well, I don't know anybody." The next time you would need meat, he would not have any for you. So you go and get busy to find somebody who will fix his transmission. But you might not find somebody who is fixing transmissions. You might find somebody who needs a new television. You know somebody who is selling televisions, and that guy knows somebody who is fixing transmissions. So, you zigzag your way back to your butcher. In the meantime, a number of people end up being satisfied with products or services that are not normally on the market. You will have meat or at least much better meat. Of course, you still must pay for it. All this trading is just to be able to buy what you need. Everybody gets something – and the butcher gets his car fixed. This system is really awful because not all the people were able to operate like this. Old people were totally out of luck. They didn't have any connections or energy so they were just plain poor. There were long lines of old ladies in front of butcher stores from very early in the morning, two hours before the stores opened, so they could get a little bit of decent meat. Even so, many times they didn't get much anyway.

So, now back to the house. I finally had electricity and my own water. I had a basement dug out. And I was actually building the house. But I came across another obstacle. Another obstacle the people here in the United States might not understand is that I needed some wood. I needed a lot of lumber and couldn't get it in the lumber yards. So, I went to the forest and through a friend, I made a connection to the forester. I asked if I could buy and chop down some trees. But they were not interested in making money on me – they needed something more. They needed to clean out the forest from the nasty winter of 1969. There had been heavy snow, which had broken the tops of a lot of trees. They needed to get rid of those trees because eventually they would die, and the insects would attack them and that would have been a disaster for the forest. So they offered me to trade trees that I needed in return for my work. I was told, "You can select the trees that you need out of the broken trees that you cut down." But the problem was that there were many times more trees to be cut down than I needed. It wasn't just cutting down the trees. That wouldn't have been that difficult. They also required me to skin the bark of every tree and cut branches off and put them on the burn piles. They showed me a huge area of forest that they wanted me to clean. I was not able to say that I was going to go for their deal because physically, I was not capable of doing that. It was too much and my mood changed quickly knowing that I wouldn't get anywhere with this deal. I went home very depressed and told my friends about this, and they said, "Oh, George, take the deal. We will help you." I told them I would not be able to pay them, but they said jokingly, "Oh, you do not have to pay us. Just buy us a bottle of whiskey." They were excited and anxious to help. They convinced me, so I agreed and we went to work. For one month we were logging. I was commuting every day after work from Prague – and on weekends. Combining logging with truck driving was exhausting. The car I was using for commuting was an old clunker, a 1936 Praga. I was so tired that one time, when I was driving in the late evening back to Prague with a car full of friends, we arrived and I had no idea how I had gotten there. Everyone else was sleeping and somehow we made it back to the city in one piece. But I had no memory of getting there! I must have had a built-in autopilot.

The land we were logging was a large parcel on a steep hillside, roughly 60 acres. We had only handsaws and axes. Chain saws were very expensive and only professional loggers had them. They didn't have to buy them since the chain saws were government property.

Father and me taking a break.

One of our friends literally moved into the forest, made a bunker out of branches, and camped there for a week like a cave man. He thought it was really cool. I tell you, it was very, very nice of those guys to help me as much as they could. We were young, and we had quite a bit of fun working together. At the end of it, I didn't have to pay them. They were just happy to help me. What good friends I had!

In the end we had this beautiful wood. We selected the best logs for the house. I made a deal with a local sawmill. I approached the shift supervisor and asked if he could help me. I explained that I was in the process of building my own house and that I was logging for this wood and now I needed lumber out of it. I made it very clear that I will pay him and his crew. He liked this proposition because the money was going to go directly into their pockets. I had already made my list of lumber that I needed. Since there would have been no time to do the work after a regular shift, the crew had to come in on the weekend. As a matter of fact, I ended up with a lot more lumber than I started with. In addition to a huge load of my long trees, I brought many short pieces only six feet long which couldn't be cut in the cutter the way it was set up. These pieces had to be sandwiched between two long logs supplied by the supervisor of the mill. When the short pieces were spit out, a lot of additional lumber came with them that I was able to keep. In the end I had a huge load of nice, beautiful long wood. That's the way I got the lumber.

Of course, I had to age it a little bit since I was also making 17 doors from scratch. The lumber for the roof structure didn't have to be aged. I also used the aged wood for the stairways and the stairway railings. I would like to mention a little bit about those doors as well as the garage door I made. I could have bought plain stock doors (if I would have paid under the table!) but since I was building the whole house by myself from scratch, I wanted these doors to be a little more stylish, a little bit better.

To make the doors, I needed a table saw and a mill. Of course, I didn't have those machines but since I had already made a welder, I constructed a machine that was half table saw and half mill. It was huge. When the machine was upright, it was a table saw. When it was flipped on its side, it was a mill. I always wanted to have my doors like those in the castles – made out of tongue and groove boards placed at a 45-degree angle. I thought those doors looked really cool. For some of the doors I needed glass panels so the light would go through, for instance in the hallway. The garage door was totally different. I don't want to brag, but I designed this door a way that nobody had seen before. The whole door was one solid piece that slid in vertical and horizontal tracks with four ball bearings in the corners of the door. You could open it very easily all the way to the ceiling with the help of a very heavy counter weight on the opposite side of the garage. The door was connected to the weight with steel cables going over pulleys right next to the ceiling. Everyone who saw this door liked it and wanted me to patent the idea. Well, I never patented it, which was probably a good thing, because about 15 years ago, I saw a similar door in one old house in the U.S. I was not the only one who had this idea.

It was interesting to work on this entire project. It took me six years to build the whole house. In six years, I went from a parcel without any water, electricity, or sewer anywhere – to a beautifully finished house that, I think, people would be proud of even here in the United States. I truly and honestly built it from SCRATCH, something that only a few do-it-yourself folks would appreciate. I thought I would be living there with my family for a lifetime, but after living there and enjoying it for six years, I had to escape and leave it all behind. I will eventually explain the reasons behind that.

Finished house.

Finished house with lots of colorful stonework on the house – chimney, fence, wall.

12

Job Upgrade

A s I mentioned so many times before, my job was to drive large trucks. I did this job during the entire construction of the house. Many times I was hauling sand, gravel, dirt, coal – not a very interesting job, but it was all right. However, it was also convenient to do this when I was building the house. Sometimes I was working with the crane operators who were loading my truck with such things as concrete panels, lumber, pipes, pallets of bricks as well as many various things like large equipment, machinery, etc. I always admired crane operators for their skills, and I wished that someday I could have that job. To me it was very interesting work with new and different challenges every day. It was also a lot better pay. I made this

Unloading heavy equipment using four cranes. Mine is front right.

as my goal, and when I finished the house, I eventually worked my way up and became a crane operator.

Talking about challenges, I would like to mention one episode I had as a crane operator. It was actually a challenge I created for myself. My partner was sick one day and I was running the crane by myself. I was dispatched to work in a very busy industrial part of Prague, installing new heavy water pipes that were replacing an old water line. These new pipes were supposed to fit into a deep, two-block long trench. This trench was running down the middle of a sidewalk next to a fence surrounding a large factory. The gate to the factory was very fancy, with a gatehouse and uniformed guards. Two large flags flew on each side of the gate, one Czech and one Russian. The gate was open to traffic that was to travel temporarily across large steel plates covering the trench. When I saw that Russian flag, I immediately made a plan that this flag would not be the same after my job was done. While I was putting pipes into the trench, I was getting closer to the gate and started to monitor these two flags very closely. I very carefully moved the crane boom around the Czech flag, but when I was close to the Russian flag, I had my chance to prove to myself how skilled an operator I really was. This had to look like a perfectly innocent accident. I moved the boom so close to the Russian flag that the flag got caught by the moving cable and dragged into the very greasy pulley way above my head. But, I had to keep looking down to the trench where workers were fitting the pipes together. I knew that I had hooked the Russian flag on the cable but of course, I ignored that fact. All of a sudden, both gate guards ran out and started yelling at me, "Look what you are doing! Look what you did!" I knew exactly what I was doing, and I was hoping that flag would come out of my pulley shredded and dirty. I acted surprised and unwound the flag from the pulley. It looked even "better" than I was expecting, black grease all over it, shredded and hanging high! Many people on the street and factory workers saw this and I could tell by their smiles, that they liked this disgraced look of that flag. The guards were still yelling at me and I said, "I'm sorry. It was an accident." But in my mind was just the opposite. I was looking at the flag and saying to myself, "That's how we feel about you Russians!" I didn't exactly feel proud of myself, but I sure felt a little bit satisfied.

13

Failures of the Communist System

I remember one time I had a terrible toothache and went to see the dentist. The communists were telling the whole world that medical treatment in their society was for free. But it didn't work that way. We already talked about that before. "Free" doesn't exist and especially under a very corrupt regime. To survive, you must pay under the table. So, I went to the dentist and I was waiting my turn in the waiting room. When my turn came I told the nurse my name and that I had a toothache. She opened the appointment book (by the way, it was in March). She said, "OK, we'll make an appointment in August." My whole face was swollen. And I said, "But I have a toothache now." She turned the book to me and asked in a very nasty way, "Do you see any opening before August?" I knew what I needed to do. I went to the bathroom, went through my wallet and put the equivalent to $100 in my hand. I went back to the office and asked to speak to the doctor directly. After a while, he came out and as I shook his hand, I stuck the $100 in his hand. He said, "Oh, come on in, Mr. Stastny. Let's see what's wrong with your tooth." The nurse, who had just told me she had no appointment was now just humming and all nice. She was a completely different person.

The dentist did the necessary work to fix my tooth and as I was leaving the building – the clinic – and was on the stairway, I felt somebody was tapping on my shoulder. It was the dentist. He said very quietly so nobody could hear, "Mr. Stastny, I heard you tell my nurse when she was asking about your personal information that you work for a construction company. I have a favor to ask of you. I am doing some remodeling in my home and I need 200 bricks. Please, can you help me?" At this point I still needed this dentist because I had to go for a later appointment to finish my tooth. I couldn't say no to him. I told the dentist that I didn't have any access to bricks. And as a crane operator, I really didn't. But I told him I would do my best and I asked him how to get in touch with him. He drew me a map to his house. If he had asked me for some steel cable or hooks, as a crane operator, I would have had access to that. I started to think about who would help me get some bricks. The next day, when I was on the job, I went to the foreman, who knew where the bricks were and could handle them. And I asked, "Hey, Lada, yesterday I went to see about my tooth and the dentist needs 200 bricks. Where can I get (steal!) them? I will pay you for them." He replied, "Is he is good dentist?" I answered, "Yeah, he fixed my tooth." And Lada said, "Forget paying me. How about we give him 400 bricks and he will be my dentist, too."

So, this is the free medical system in a socialistic society. It's the same with the rest of the freebies like free education, free retirement, etc. If anybody here in the U.S. suggests to provide some services for free, please remember, it will not be free and quality will be lost. All this free business will collapse eventually – and the whole society will collapse. I am not saying this because it is some kind of hypothetical theory. It is my experience. It becomes very simple when I try to explain it. Humans are naturally lazy. I don't mean to put people down. It is in our nature – we were born that way. People will not work if they don't have to work – in any society. If you don't have to work – if you find $1,000 every week in your mailbox – you will do nothing. You will play – golf, hobbies, vacation or something. But somebody has to put the money in your mailbox. Somebody pays for it. So, this was the trend of people in that communist society. They knew they could get away with cheating. And then a chain, an avalanche, happened. It takes one person, in theory, to collapse the whole system. Even if you will educate people to be honest, there will always be somebody who will start to cheat. Other cheaters will see this and then there will be a whole army of cheaters. If we have a free medical system, I can go to the doctor and fake that I am sick. The doctor lets me stay home and the government will also pay me just like I was working. What a deal! Many people will say, "Great! Let's be sick!" I will explain this with a simple example.

Let's say you are a ditch digger. They tell you in the morning, "You are starting here and by evening, you have to be at the end of this block. Here is the shovel. Start." You are digging with this other guy who is digging another ditch next to you. This guy digs for a couple of hours and then he just throws down the shovel. He goes to the doctor and says, "I have a backache." The doctor shows him that he doesn't have any available appointments so the guy gives him $100 and then magically, there is an opening. The doctor gives the guy some medicine and a slip to excuse him from work for a couple of weeks. The doctor takes care of the guy because he gave him $100. He tells him to stay home and rest. But in the meantime, you are still digging. The shovel of your friend is still lying there. You don't like it because you know that he is just staying home, faking being sick and most likely smoking cigars and watching TV – and he is being paid. So you are digging, and after the third day, you are blocks from his shovel. And you are thinking, "I am an idiot." So you go to the doctor and with $100 in your hand as a bribe, you tell him you have a blister on your ankle or a stomachache, or something else. And it goes just like that. Pretty soon, everybody is faking being sick. But naturally, sometimes some people really get sick. And on top of all of the cheaters, these really sick people also have to pay under the table to doctors or they wouldn't be seen like me with my toothache. This corrupt government is running the show. The government is controlling everything – doctors' offices, military, public transportation, large and small businesses and everybody is cheating. Pretty soon everybody has the same work attitude and work ethic. Nobody wants to work. It comes down to faking, cheating, and the attitude, "Give me, give me, give me!" The whole economy will collapse! I know that I'm repeating myself when I'm saying "People are just people." You can educate them as much as you want and still most will cheat. Even in this country, if a company provides its employees with sick leave, there will always be someone who misuses it. Sick leave is for being sick. But be honest now, you have to admit that it has gotten pretty common to use sick leave for extending weekends, taking the car for service, helping somebody to move furniture, etc. Look at how many people are cheating on their taxes. People in high government positions are, from time to time, caught avoiding paying taxes or not paying enough. It means to me, if you catch one person, there are many who don't get caught. Just like with speeding on the highway. You know that you should not speed, but almost everyone is speeding with only a few getting caught. I speed too, but that will not collapse the economy. If there would be "dirty" cops taking bribes, that would definitely be the decline of a good society.

The socialistic way screwed up and ruined everything that was successful and pretty. In my opinion, with socialism, this will happen anywhere in the world. Even though these communists were bragging to the whole world about their achievements, these achievements were the successes of smart and hard working businessmen who started and developed productive companies. Communists are only really responsible for destroying what had been so successful before they took over. In my opinion, socialism cannot work because of the promises of a lot of freebies. I am a great believer in the reward system and the only free thing I believe in is free enterprise.

As you can readily see from my story, I am describing how socialism cannot start from nothing and build up. Socialism can start only from taking over something that is already built up, running it down and destroying it in the process, and ending up with nothing. In Czechoslovakia, it took 41 years, but it happened. I experienced and lived through socialism for 32 years of my life. So, I hope that even socialistic believers will give me a little bit of courtesy and credit, so I can talk about this. You can educate and educate, and many people will still want to cheat, take short cuts, and get a free ride. For instance, look at any super market or discount store at how many shopping carts are left in the parking lots without being returned to where they belong. This example doesn't involve anything, just a few extra steps. Instead the thinking is, "If I don't have to do it and can get away with it, I will!" These people know what is right and what is wrong, but they just don't care. They think only about what is best for them. Now can you imagine how many people will take advantage of free medical instead of thinking twice, "Do I really need it?" Many people will storm the ERs and doctors' offices even if they don't really need it, knowing that they don't have to pay for any of this service. On top of this, who do they think is going to pay for it and pay them for missing work?

I think it might be appropriate to mention something that my parents taught me. I believe it is a very basic and logical rule – "If you don't work, you don't eat. If you don't have money, you don't buy." To me it is very simple and clear. If you follow this rule, you don't get into trouble. I heard over the years that some people complain about many things or even about life, that life is too hard. In my opinion, there's nothing wrong with "hard." "Hard" makes you a better person. "Easy" makes you a wimp! Some people might think that I'm too harsh or too radical because life really isn't so easy. My argument to that is, "If you are healthy, don't make any excuses. Get off your butt and do something about it! Don't make it complicated!"

So we had this society where you could not buy meat, toilet paper, tires for your car, and millions of other things if you didn't have a connection. So, what was this vision of communism? They were preaching that someday everybody is going to be so honest and such hard workers and everything in the stores will be free, too. That's the goal of the communist society. They said we are going to be so educated and so honest with each other that we would not need any money – money would not exist. They claimed we would work really hard for eight hours every day, and then on the way home we would stop by the store and get only what we needed. It would be there for free for us. Communism is a very beautiful dream that will never work because it is a utopia. Look at what the communists achieved with this utopia – just the opposite. It will never, ever work because people are people. There will always be one guy who will throw down the shovel and say he has a backache. And it will start an avalanche. I am convinced of that. There is nothing that is free.

Please, I don't mean to be making a political speech. I love the United States, and I very strongly believe that BOTH of our political parties are very important. They should monitor each other, promote the best, most reasonable and realistic ideas from both sides, and put them to work. Any politician running for office – and I don't care what party they represent – who promises something for free, I think they just want to say something attractive to get people's votes. I would say to them, "You can't be serious or you are out of your mind. We are not that naïve." I'm just telling you how it works. It's not going to happen – especially it is not going to work for jobs at the lower level. The lower the job you have, the more motivated you will be to abuse this free system, starting with food stamps, free this and free that. I very strongly believe in the reward system. You are rewarded when you provide something of value.

So that's what I think is the best system and that is what I have found here in the U.S. I love this country. Believe me, I know there are many problems here. People are complaining (also part of human nature – to complain) about how expensive things are, how difficult life is. But I wish that these complainers would go to some other countries, no matter where on this planet, and have to live there for a few years. I can guarantee you they would be very happy to come back here and the complaining would stop. This is truly the land of opportunity – you can be whatever you want to be, do whatever you want to do. You can do nothing, but the consequences would be your fault, or you can go as far or as high as you want.

14

Decision to Escape

O ur new house was on the outskirts of Prague, actually in a little town. I could walk to the edge of Prague and to the last city bus stop, at the edge of the city transportation. Our house was finished and we were enjoying it a lot. Upstairs I built a music room that was furnished with a piano and many stringed instruments. We held many good jam sessions there with many good and enthusiastic musicians. Sometimes we played all night, having a fantastic time, and in the morning we went to work without any sleep. Well, I guess we felt that we were indestructible.

Jam session in the music room of the finished house. From left: my father, myself, brother Jaroslav, our good friend Honza Zajicek.

I wanted to get involved in our little community with recreational activities for young people. The group of young people in this town didn't do much for themselves. They were involved with drinking beer and visiting, not doing anything productive, nothing that I would call good quality free time. I was young, full of energy, looking at these kids and thinking, "We need to do something better here." And I thought, "Let's build a volleyball court and play." There was an old reservoir covered with weeds and brush that provided extra water for the fire department. But it was really for the frogs. Next to it was an ugly piece of dirt. I suggested, "We can level it and I can bring some sand." I had access to a truck since I was working for the construction company. The young people got excited. We worked a number of evenings and a few weekends making quite a beautiful volleyball court out of this totally neglected area. We made poles for the net, benches for sitting and bought a ball. People were not very good volleyball players, but we had fun. More and more young people came and joined us. And we started to do more things. We talked to the mayor – asking if the town would clean up the neglected reservoir, so we could use it as a swimming pool. I proposed to the mayor that the fire department could still use the clean water from the swimming pool. They didn't have to have dirty water. The citizens could swim in this clean reservoir and have fun. I had to be persistent, but when this was eventually accomplished, needless to say, folks of all ages had fun, and I became a popular person in this town.

There was a city meeting held by the communists, and this is an interesting and important point in my story. There were going to be elections, like here, to vote for a new government. The communists wanted to be elected. But you didn't really have a choice to vote for anybody else. The whole thing was just a formality, a total fake, so they could say they had been elected or actually re-elected. They wanted to tell the citizens what kind of achievements they had accomplished and what they had planned for the next term.

It was the first time I had attended something like this since I was so busy building the house. Really, I was not very interested in some communist meeting and their blobbling. But I thought maybe I would hear something interesting there. So I went. There were about 400 people attending. These communist leaders were sitting at the front on a stage. Some were big shots from Prague and some were local. They started talking about their achievements. Then they started saying what they were going to do for us during the next term.

The communist leaders said they were going to repaint the tall metal towers for high-voltage electricity. They were saying how many megawatts of electricity went through these towers. I was listening to this for a while. Then I stood up and said, "Excuse me, guys, but can you do something better for us? You are going to repaint those big towers. That is not going to improve our lives." They asked, "What do you think you would like for us to do?" I said, "Well, for instance, when we are standing at the bus stop early in the morning, we are standing in the rain and the mud since it isn't paved. How about making a nice clean and covered waiting area?" All the citizens were applauding this as a good idea. And then I told them that sometimes the buses just didn't show up – or they went right past us because, being the last stop on the line, they were often full. Then we would have to begin to walk to work, getting there very late. So, I asked them to make a nice waiting room, something that would be also pleasant to look at, something that would make us proud of our environment. I asked them to make sure the buses would be on time, so we could get to work. I emphasized, "The new paint on the high voltage towers really doesn't excite us!" As a result of my simple requests, these communist leaders did nothing but make excuses for their inaction and instead began questioning just who I was. The local citizens were on my side and got fired up, but I got into trouble. These leaders weren't used to being questioned or criticized by someone brave enough to speak up.

Now it is important to mention that the last communist president of Czechoslovakia was Gustav Husak. I don't think he was a significant figure in our Czech history. He was kind of a stick in the mud, jumping when the big boys in Moscow whistled (I mean Brezhnev and his gang). He never smiled and always looked too serious and kind of upset. Nobody really liked Husak, but he was the one who was often bragging about being the patron saint of our part of Prague. This section of the city was very industrialized, and he was always hollering that we are the future, that we and our Russian brothers would create the modern society of the future. He claimed that we would be on a pedestal that would be an example for better tomorrows. To me, these were just empty communist slogans and we were still standing in the rain and mud hoping that we would be picked up by an overcrowded bus. So when I stood up and said what I said about improving the bus stops, the communists just looked at me and said, "And just how would you do that?" I said, "What would be so difficult for you to contact President Gustav Husak because he is the sponsor for this part of the industrial city – and just point out our problems. I'm sure Comrade Gustav Husak would be very happy to help and take care of us and we would all actually benefit out of it." Everyone in the audience of this meeting was clapping and cheering...

The people on the platform who were not local leaders, who were big shots from Prague, were just pointing to each other and pointing to me – wondering, "Who is this guy?" They were writing down my name. Then, one of the big shots from the communist committee said, "Comrade George Stastny, you shouldn't criticize us. I understand that you have a beautiful house because we communists, we leaders, we are taking good care of you. We are providing the best things for you. It is by our doing that you have such a nice home. Because we are here, we are in power, and without us you would not have that house." That really made me angry. I stood up very fast and said, "Without you I would have had the house a lot faster. The only things I got from you were obstacles in the places that you are supposed to be in charge of..." That was another thing I said that got me into trouble. But everyone was just cheering me on. They were clapping loudly and saying, "George, just go for it." They were roaring. I was 35, and it was 1979. Can you imagine that after six years of working like a slave to build a house, that these dirty crooks, the communists, were taking credit for it? It was too much for me. I lost my cool with my comments because I had had it with all of the empty promises and lies. I couldn't be polite to them anymore. I felt like a hero and I wasn't afraid of them. I was young, probably dumb and gullible, and I quickly realized that by standing up to them, I was paying a huge price.

Two days after this meeting, I started to see a couple of guys in a car focusing on our house from a distance. I realized that I was being watched. This went on for days. I knew they were undercover police, just waiting for me to take a wrong step. Or maybe they were only harassing me. So, I decided to go and ask them if they had run out of gas to harass them a little bit, too. When I was almost within talking distance, they started to back up, went around the area and watched me from another angle on a different road. I knew then that I was in trouble.

To go back to the time when I was working for the construction company, one of the bosses was a piano player. Unfortunately, he was a communist, but he was a good piano player. Remember I told you that in the military we often played sports or music with communists. Communists were always all around us. It was like bad weather – you couldn't do much about it. You had to live with it and sometimes, get the best out of it. Well, a similar thing existed in my work. This boss wanted to play music with me. This guy really liked me, and one time he really opened up and confessed to me, "George, I am just being a communist because I was unhappy with my previous job and because I want to do this particular job, I am required to be a member of the Communist Party." I didn't like this reason but I felt like I was being cornered, so I had to put up with this answer and get the best out of it. I didn't play music with him every day. Maybe a couple of times or so. But he felt he was my friend. I was always distant, but I played with him.

Anyway, the important thing now is that he came to me a few days after the town communist meeting, and he said, "George, I am putting my safety on the line. I should not be talking to you, but you are being watched. You are being watched everywhere you go." I had a pretty good idea already but I didn't know I was being watched everywhere. And I didn't know he also knew about my trouble. He knew from a totally different source, and it was very serious. Yes, it was very serious, but it created something else inside of me. I had had it with living this type of life under communism. In public, pretending that everything was fine and inside feeling so frustrated. I was 35 years old and for all these years, since I was a little boy, the communists had forced me to go through a lot of trouble and problems. I had had to constantly zigzag between communist lies and harassment. I felt so hurt and frustrated. It was the straw that "broke the camel's back," knowing that we were under constant surveillance. I got so, SO sick of it that I made a radical decision. I came home that night and told my wife, Helena, how I felt and at that time, calmly, I told her, "This is getting very hot, dangerous and ridiculous. We have only two options. We can stay where we are and wait to make a wrong move (like paying under the table or something else illegal). There is no way we can live 100% honestly in this corrupt regime. They are waiting for us to make a wrong move and then we will end up in jail. Or we must get out of here!"

These words sounded like a big bomb! We had our own family as well as an extended family and many friends. We had just recently finished building our new house. These were extremely important and serious issues. Just thinking about this was making me dizzy and cold! Then I got specific and told Helena, "I know this is not going to be easy, but the smartest option is to make up our minds and escape from this country." What followed was a long silence. Our eyes were wide open and you could hear only our deep breaths. The word "escape" is easy to say, but in reality, it is very difficult to do and to escape from a communist country, to escape from behind the Iron Curtain was an incredibly huge deal. Helena looked at me and asked,

"Where would we go?" I answered, "To America! We will start a new life in the United States and of course, we are taking our boys with us." Escaping like that, with the whole family, was like telling someone I was going to go to the moon – or winning the Power Ball jackpot. That big of a decision required us to think about it and to think very carefully! This decision would be a life or death decision. It was the middle of 1979, and everybody knew it was impossible to escape through the Iron Curtain, but definitely incredibly impossible to escape with an entire family.

But we had no choice, so we started to make plans for an escape...

15

Secret and Dangerous Preparations

The plans were top secret. We couldn't tell anybody. I mean nobody! Not even the closest members of our family. Not brothers, sisters, parents, anybody. First of all we didn't want to jeopardize their safety. If we were caught, they would be punished also. And secondly, for our safety – because the more people who would know, the bigger the chance that we would be discovered.

I knew of other cases where people got caught trying to escape. When they got caught, the communists put them on the TV. They publicized this to scare others. Then these people were tried publicly. So even though we were both very scared, my wife Helena agreed that it was our only choice. We saw there was no way for us to adapt to being constantly harassed and pretend that we were happy. We couldn't stop this trouble and get ourselves out of it.

We began to make our plans. We had no idea what this decision represented. We did not know where to start. We felt very overwhelmed, confused, scared, but we had to overcome these negative feelings and start to think positively, realistically and practically. We were thinking of what to take, what to leave behind, what it would cost and many other things. This was a very complex plan, that in the beginning, I had only a partial idea of how difficult it would eventually get. And it did – it really snowballed.

I knew it was going to be difficult, but I had no idea... If I had been escaping by myself, it would have been so much easier. But that was unthinkable. We needed to do this with the whole family. It cost a lot of money – to be paid under the table at the right places at the right time. I never knew who was going to take my money and turn me in afterwards. Of course, there was no literature of any kind or brochure to pick up in a bookstore or government office on "How to Escape." It was all done by putting little pieces together and trying to make a picture out of it. But try to make a picture out of rumors. You would hear one thing from someone and something completely different from someone else.

I knew we were living inside of a fence – that we were surrounded by an Iron Curtain on all sides bordering with the free world. There was no Iron Curtain as such, but guarded borders nevertheless, between Poland and Czechoslovakia, or Russia and Czechoslovakia, or Hungary and Czechoslovakia. But there was an Iron Curtain on the borders of Czechoslovakia with West Germany and with Austria. We were surrounded. We couldn't go to the free side of the world. We just couldn't get out.

I feel I need to explain, especially for the younger generations, just what the Iron Curtain really was. Many people in the free world thought that this was just a hypothetical line between communist countries and the free world. ABSOLUTELY NOT! The Iron Curtain WAS NOT hypothetical. It was a very real and ugly fence 20 feet tall, 20 feet thick, made out of coiled barbed wire with guard towers, night lighting, land mines, guard dogs, concrete barriers. There was all military power that you can imagine

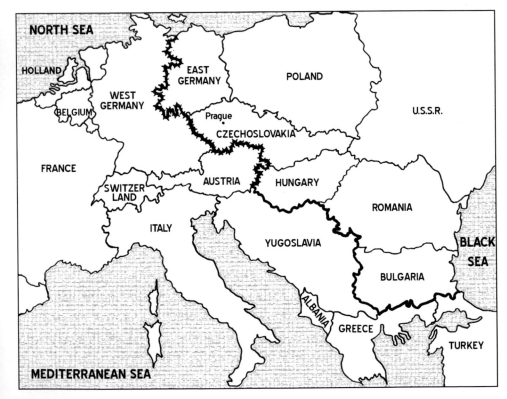

The Iron Curtain divides Europe – communist countries were cut off from the free world in 1946

– tanks, helicopters, machine guns, etc. The same military power was placed at the borders between Hungary and Yugoslavia, Romania and Yugoslavia, and Bulgaria and Yugoslavia. But there was no physical fence so nobody could call it the "Iron Curtain," but it was basically the same thing. The simple reason for all that was the Russians didn't want to lose population from the more advanced satellite countries next to Russia. They didn't want to let anyone from a communist country escape to the free world through Yugoslavia. Yugoslavia hadn't joined either NATO or the Warsaw Pact. If somebody from any communist countries would be able to get to Yugoslavia, then it would have been an easy step to Austria or Italy. And there were some lucky people who were able to escape like that.

I had never seen the Iron Curtain. As ordinary citizens, we were never allowed to go see it. We were not even allowed to say there was an Iron Curtain. But there were people who worked there, or lived close by, so sooner or later the word got out. There were Czech soldiers who were in the military for two years as guards for the Iron Curtain. Even though they were politically screened, they still talked. When their service ended, they talked to their friends and families. So the Iron Curtain became a very public "secret."

Now I need to explain that something very incredible and important happened with the timing of our plans to escape. As a crane operator I was assigned to transfer some equipment from a West German truck to a Czechoslovakian truck at the border. It was large equipment for building roads. I had no idea in advance that I would actually be able to see the Iron Curtain. I showed up for work in the morning, like any other day and on the job order was "Border Crossing Cheb" between West Germany and Czechoslovakia at a designated time. Our crew was made up of three people with two people on the crane (my partner and myself) and one person driving a big truck.

I just couldn't believe the coincidence. To me it was absolutely incredible – the timing couldn't have been better. We took off from Prague and headed west in the direction of the border. We had a special piece of paper with the job order proving to all the guards that we were authorized to be doing this job. As we were getting closer, we were stopped so many times. Approximately ten km from the border, there was the first checkpoint. We had to stop and tell the soldiers why we were going toward the border. After another five km, there was another check point. The check points became more frequent the closer we got. Finally, when we were close enough that we could see the border – maybe 600 feet – there was an interesting set up. There was a gigantic roadblock. It wasn't the physical border crossing yet, but it was the beginning of the Iron Curtain. It was a gate that was preventing people from getting crazy ideas, like using a big truck or a big tank and crashing through the Iron Curtain. This "gate" consisted of two tremendously large offset concrete blocks connected by a large iron beam. Each block was the size of a house, one block on each side of the highway. The iron beam was three feet tall and two feet thick. The beam was actually welded together with a number of steel I-beams and was blocking the road at an angle. Because it was at an angle, there was no way to break through, even with a tank. You would just slide off and crash into the opposite concrete block. Soldiers were opening and closing the iron beam electrically. From this distance, we could see the real border, the fences and barbed wire. We could also see the guard towers with soldiers using heavy machine guns, searchlights, floodlights and guard dogs. It was overwhelming. Not even a mouse could get through. It would be impossible.

Now, at the last stop before the border, at this huge iron beam gate, they checked our papers again. They called to see if the German trucks were there waiting for us, but they were not. We were told we would have to wait and were instructed to pull over to the side of the barrier. It turned out that Germany was playing soccer with Holland that day, so the Germans never showed up. Instead, the German truckers were watching soccer, which is very popular in Europe. Finally a guard informed us that the Germans would come the next day.

We were sitting in the crane waiting, and my partner was sleeping all night. But I was watching. I was watching how it works at night, and it was so fascinating. I was realizing more and more there was no way to escape, even at night. There were lights going on all night long. Sirens going off all the time. For instance, if a deer would walk by, motion detectors would trigger the sirens that would go off. There was a lake close by. The Iron Curtain was even going through the water. There were military boats patrolling the water. Radar controlling the air space was everywhere. You would have to see it to believe it. While we were just sitting there, I was watching what was going on. Since we were sitting next to this iron beam, I noticed that the soldiers were opening this gate only as much as was necessary for a vehicle to get through. When someone came by on a motorcycle, they opened the gate only a small bit. If a car came by, they opened it a bit more. They never opened it more than was necessary. And, of course, they were using the same routine when people were coming from Germany. But, again, just as much as was needed. It was an interesting, very important and valuable learning experience for me. Sitting there I realized that our escape plans had to be perfected down to the last detail.

The next day the German truckers finally arrived. We were allowed to move our crane and truck to the actual border. It was a very weird and exciting feeling for me. I couldn't conceive of the fact that I was just a few steps from the free world. But at the same time, I knew that I couldn't do anything about it because my family was not with me. We started to transfer equipment from the German trucks to our truck. We were being watched by the guards very carefully until we finished and left. Every single move and step.

While we were working, I watched how the guards were searching one Czech car that was in the process of crossing the border to West Germany. I witnessed what an extensive search was being conducted. Everything in the interior of the car, including the contents of the trunk, had to be removed. They searched the engine compartment, under the car, removed the hubcaps, spare tire and jack, carpets, floor mats. They went through all the luggage. The passengers were searched thoroughly. For me to see this was a very scary but important experience. I need to mention that the border crossing between communist Czechoslovakia and free West Germany was nothing like the border crossing between the U.S. and Canada or Mexico. At these crossings, drivers experience long lines with hundreds of vehicles waiting to cross. At this Czech border crossing there may have been one vehicle in an hour, giving the border guards plenty of time to completely disassemble the car if they chose to, and they did!

When I came back home, I was telling Helena all about this. I told her there was no way to fly over, dig under, or shoot my way through. There was no way. I knew we would have to figure out something different and very clever. She agreed with me and knew how important it was to keep our plans completely secret. She supported me 100%. She was very good at that. She took care of the kids – keeping them happy and making sure they did not have any idea what we were planning. The boys were six and eight, and it would have been very easy for them to say something to the neighbors' kids. We had to be so careful.

I couldn't tell a soul. I had to keep my family completely out of it. But we needed to make a plan. I did get to a couple of roadblocks along the way that I couldn't get around without getting help from someone I trusted. I had to share my plans with a couple of people because I needed their help. I selected them very carefully. We never said anything to anyone in my family or Helena's family for their safety.

I thought about this escape scheme day and night, and then I made a simple plan that later started to get more and more complicated. The whole plot was based on telling the authorities that our son had a health issue and therefore we needed to go on a vacation to Italy for three weeks. But they wouldn't know we would never come back. Of course, we had to come up with a reason that the whole family had to go with him to Italy. Remember, the communist rule was that no one could leave the country. But if they ever allowed anyone to leave, only one or two family members could go to the West. The rest of the family had to remain behind the Iron Curtain as hostages, insurance that the person would come back.

We made up a story that our oldest son had a lung problem, and that he needed to get out of the city environment and the pollution, that he needed to breathe warm, fresh sea air. And since Czechoslovakia doesn't have any seashore, the closest place with warm, fresh sea air was to go to Italy. "Warm" was an important word because the authorities could have sent us to East Germany or Poland to the North Sea. But we needed a doctor's recommendation. So, we had to find and pay some doctor to give this medical diagnosis and statement to us. When I finally found this doctor, I had to put on a really good act so the doctor wouldn't suspect anything was wrong and would really think that we were going on this health mission. He thought he was giving a recommendation we all needed to go because of our son's young age. He had no idea we were not coming back. I paid him well to say that this trip was necessary for all of us. If somebody had later come back to the doctor, he could honestly say there was no way he knew. Since our son really did have a problem with his lungs sometime earlier and there was a record of that, we used this excuse as the pillar of our plan. But we had to convince the doctor to say that our vacation to the beach as a family was absolutely and critically necessary as part of our son's treatment.

We had to be so secretive. It was almost unbelievable. Helena's mother was living just a few blocks from us, and we saw her on an almost daily basis. She was also helping us a lot when we were building the house. We were surrounded with neighbors who were our friends. Our kids played together. Everybody knew everything about everybody. But we had to do all of this very secretly. I know that I am repeating myself, but I am trying to emphasize, we couldn't even tell anyone that we were planning a vacation to Italy.

As it turned out, it took over a year to make the necessary plans. This wasn't something that could happen overnight or in just a few weeks, like a normal vacation. We knew when we got to the border that we would have to look to the officials like we really were going on a vacation to Italy. We couldn't take the chance that we would have something with us that would be suspicious, that would cause the border guards to question us. For instance, we couldn't have too many clothes, or winter sweaters, or some sort of precious family memento. We had to have bathing suits. We had to have a tent for camping as well as a lot of other gear. We bought a large tent at one sporting goods store, but we didn't know how to put it up. We had to practice. But we couldn't just put it up in the backyard – people would ask where we were going. We had to drive far away from our house, out to the middle of nowhere, where nobody would see us so we could practice with our tent. And of course, we had to do this without the kids knowing.

Now let's talk about getting our papers in order. If you are living in the free world, you can go anywhere you want. But under the communist regime, it was different. They were telling the whole world that we were free. That we could go anywhere we wanted. Of course, this was all false. In order to travel, the process was very difficult. You had to apply and pay for a passport, which was not that difficult. In a couple of months, it would arrive in the mail. On the first page of the passport, it said, "This passport is good for the whole world," and on the next page it said, "except these countries..." And they named 40 countries that you could not go to which were those in the free world. You could go to Poland, East Germany, Romania, Bulgaria, Hungary and maybe Russia if you were lucky – if they didn't think you were going to make any trouble. On the bottom in small print, it said, "You cannot go to these 40 countries without the extension of this passport." (In Czech language "Pasova dolozka.")

To keep this simple, I am going to refer to this extension as "special page #28." So you looked for page 28, but there was no page 28. The passport was useless. To get this special page 28, you had to apply for it. To apply for this page and actually get it, was extremely difficult, almost impossible. The application for this special page, was four pages long. Each page was filled with lines where you had to get permission from special organizations or groups of people who would recommend and approve that you can go on this trip, assuming that you would come back. Each person who signed and stamped this document was "proving" that you were a good citizen, that you deserved the trip, that you were honest and that you would come back. There were more than 20 signatures required on this application for the special page 28. It started on line one with the Communist Party. There were several signatures required just for the party. For example, one of signatures I needed was from the guy at Tesla, the electronics factory, who wanted me to join the party, and to whom I had said "No." Then came the Workers' Union that in a communist country is almost like the Communist Party itself. There really isn't a big difference. They always worked together and were basically the same bunch of creeps and losers, but unfortunately, with a lot of power. I also needed permission from the military since I was registered in the active reserves.

As I was turning through these pages, I thought, "This is impossible." Then I slept on it, and I knew that we had to go through this and that I must do it. If any one of these required signatures had said, "No," we would not have been allowed to go anywhere. Even the city librarian had to sign for us! There were people in the neighborhood that were communist, and they had some kind of job to watch over everything and everybody, just to be nosy for the party. And I had to get their signatures. Those people were the worst people. If I didn't say every morning, "Good morning, Comrade Novak," I would never get the signature. I had to play sneaky games with everybody. And I had to pay a lot under the table – especially when I hit a roadblock. Remember this was a society of corruption. To get these signatures, I needed to have a lot more money than we had. So we decided we had to sell our house – secretly. I knew that this was going to happen, so I had already started to work on the sale of our new house. It sounds so easy but it was NOT EASY AT ALL! Just to make this decision was very difficult. Imagine building a new house from scratch for six years and then, after living in it for six years, selling it and spending all the money on something very dangerous, that after all, might not work. You wouldn't even have a place to live and you wouldn't have any money either! We needed the money out of this house to pay people off – under the table. It was really, really dangerous because you didn't know that the people you were bribing would not take your money and then turn around and report you to the communist authorities. So much work – so much trouble!!! So much risk!!!

Now about selling the house... I went to the advertising agency in downtown Prague. The office was made up of a large number of windows on which were displayed various ads of real estate for sale. Many people would stroll by these windows, reading the particulars about what was available, making notes as they read. Advertising in a newspaper was not as common at that time. I needed to ask some questions such as, "What is it going to cost me to sell the house? How soon can you advertise it? How does this agency work?" There were many people wanting information and help and only a couple of clerks working. I noticed that there was an old lady in the office who seemed to be just floating around in the crowd of customers. I didn't know if she worked there or was just helping there. I thought maybe she could give me some answers. When I walked over to her and looked at her up close, she looked kind of poor, like you would want to give her a dollar to buy a sandwich for herself. She looked like she didn't know anything about anything. Since I had already made eye contact with her, she started to talk to me and asked me what kind of house I had for sale and where it was located. I gave her the information and then mysteriously, she said, "Don't worry, I'll take care of it." I didn't think much of it. I told her that I wasn't going to advertise at that particular moment, that I had to go home and think about it. To understand what happened next, you must remember that communism is very corrupt.

The next day, a total stranger showed up at my door and said, "I hear you want to sell this house. How much do you want for it?" I asked him how he heard about the house. He said that this lady (he described the old lady perfectly) at an advertising agency gave him a tip on a good house because he had paid her under the table. He had asked her to tell him about a good house that had not yet been advertised. This guy had a lot of money – a lot of cash. He got the cash because he was what we called a gypsy. Gypsies traveled from place to place and set up stands to sell things, sort of like those little stands you see in Mexico – little stands with jewelry, T-shirts, etc. So, he was doing that. He also looked like a gypsy. Communist society actually promoted gypsies. The communists were very strongly against racism. And the gypsies were taking advantage of the situation. The communists allowed them to have these stands. And they were making a lot of money.

They didn't claim all their income. Nobody actually knew how much they really made. So, here is a guy with a lot of cash who wants my house. I made a deal with him that we would sell him and his family the house. Now I have to explain a very serious and complicated situation. We were not ready to escape. I had to make many, many arrangements that took a lot of time. At the same time, for a number of reasons, nobody could find out that we were selling the house. For one, neighbors and friends would get suspicious. We had worked on that house like slaves for a long time, and now we were selling it?

Another reason was Helena's mother who, under no circumstances, could find out because it would have broken her heart. This would have been a total disaster for her. She had helped quite a bit with the house and would immediately figure out what was going on. So I told this guy that we would sell him the house under the condition that it must be kept a secret until we had found a really great, luxurious condo in Prague. Then we could show our new condo to Helena's mother. It would not hurt her as much if she could be told about this new luxury apartment at the same time she was told that we had sold the house. It was all just a lie that I made up to buy some time. And the guy went for it. He was not the only one who went for that lie. There was the city mayor, who also had to sign the papers to sell the house. He had to certify that we were the owners and the house had been built a certain way. It was a society of signatures and stamps. But we really worried about Helena's mother. We felt sorry because we knew it was going to be very hard for her to lose us. I knew our escape was going to cause a lot of pain for everybody, but I also believed that eventually, in the long run, it would reverse to good!

I need to explain the financial process for selling a house. It was a common practice in Czechoslovakia, and it became almost the law, that houses were sold for twice as much as the fair market price. I will give you an example. We were selling a house for 200,000 krons. But we needed to get twice as much – 400,000 krons. And it was absolutely normal. We weren't being greedy. This is the way the society worked. So, the buyer was paying me 200,000 into one hand, and he would pay me another 200,000 into the other hand. The extra 200,000 was never recorded. It was not legal but everybody knew that and it was very common. No one ever sold a house for the fair market price only. So, we were doing this deal, and when we were signing the papers at the lawyer's office, the lawyer (in this case it was a lady) wanted to make sure I had gotten paid into both hands. Before she legalized the sale, she looked at me and asked, "Does this person owe you anything?" And I said, "No." And she said again and emphasized, "I mean, does he owe you anything?" He had already paid me into both hands, but there was still a 10,000 kron balance that he said he was going to give me later because he didn't have enough cash on hand. That was between us on a handshake. I let him do that because for me it was a still a good deal. I trusted him that he would pay me later, and I was happy that he had gone for the story that bought me time. So, I told the lawyer that he didn't owe me anything. I just hoped that later he would give me the balance of 10,000 krons as he had promised.

But back to the story of the required signatures. The money from the sale of the house was disappearing fast. I would like to make a long story short, but getting some of the signatures for our application to get the necessary page 28 for the passports was quite interesting, very scary and expensive. One of the signatures cost me roughly an amount equal to $50,000 today. And that was just one of the signatures.

There was one very important signature that I needed, and I didn't know how to get to this person and bribe him since he was a high-ranking police official in the Communist Party. It was a big dilemma for me, and I needed to do a lot of thinking about it. Then I figured it out. I had a friend, Jaroslav Zeman, who had been my partner on the crane in the past. He knew someone who knew someone who could lead me to the person whose signature I needed. I trusted Jaroslav with my life. We had worked together for two years, had become very good friends, and most importantly, we knew each other really well. I had helped him once when he was severely injured in a crane accident, and he always felt that he owed me a big favor. After I thought about this for a long time and very carefully, I thought it would be extremely helpful to me if I shared my secret plan with Jaroslav. I told him about it, and he helped arrange the meeting to get this signature.

The meeting was arranged (with money paid under the table) by two guys who drove me in their car in the middle of the night far from Prague. It was in an area that I was not familiar with. Nobody was talking and it was very strange. I felt very uncomfortable. I don't think we wanted to talk because we didn't know each other, but we all knew why we were there. From time to time, they mentioned. "We are almost there." I started to worry more and more if this was not some terrible mistake. Pretty soon, I noticed a few lights from a nearby house, but we were still in the middle of nowhere in a dark forest in the middle of the night.

The driver finally stopped the car and said, "We can't and shouldn't get any closer." They looked at me and said, "You stay here. Give us the money and your application. We're going to get the signature and stamp you need from this person." They also said, "This is very dangerous. The person whose signature you need cannot be seen by you and recognized under any circumstances." I will never forget what was going through my mind. I was thinking, "Should I trust them and give them my money," (which was as I said previously, like giving someone today $50,000 in cash – can you imagine that?) "or should I get out of the car and start to run for my life?" I had to make a quick decision. I was so far and deep into my preparation for escaping that I felt there was no way back. But still I had to protect myself as best I could. I had to think, "Who are these guys? Who recommended them to me? How did I get in touch with them? Is this a good decision?" I said to myself, "George, you have to go forward."

So I gave them my papers and my money, and they disappeared into the darkness. I felt like a bird, trapped in a cage waiting for the police to come and arrest me. If that would have happened, my whole future would have definitely been destroyed. I was trying to think of some explanation to give the police in case that would happen. But I couldn't think of anything realistic that could get me out of this trouble. I was sitting there probably 20-30 minutes. Every minute felt like an hour long. My head was spinning and I was sweating. I had no guarantee that those guys were not going to turn me in. Or somehow trick me. So many things were going through my mind. I just prayed for a positive outcome.

Then, finally these two guys came back. My blood pressure was sky high. They got into the car and said, "Here we go," and gave me the papers with the correct stamp and signature. GOD, WHAT A RELIEF!!! Another hurdle was cleared! Just remembering all of this is very exhausting for me!

Back to the people who bought our house. There was a law that said if you escaped, your property would be confiscated. If you sold your property before you escaped, and then escaped, and the authorities could prove that you were planning to escape, the property would be confiscated from the people who bought it from you. There was no way I would do that to someone. I couldn't live with that. I couldn't sell a house for a bunch of money and say, "To heck with you. That's not my problem anymore." I had to play a whole new game now – how to prove that I was not planning to escape.

I decided to contact Josef, a person that I used to work with a long time ago. I knew him well and knew that he was pretending to be on the communist side. I knew that he was someone I could pay off. He was the driver of a government limousine and knew many high-ranking people, and one of them was the lawyer for the son of one of the former communist presidents. Josef hooked me up with this lawyer, who (for a lot of money) promised he would be sure that he got the case after I escaped. We knew that after the authorities realized we were gone, there would be a trial without us present. And we knew that they would find us guilty of escaping from the country. Then they would determine whether we had left with the intention of escaping. This lawyer said he would make sure that these people who bought our house would not lose the property. He had the power to prove that we didn't have any intention to escape. Josef tried to assure me that he was giving me solid information, that the lawyer had a lot of power, that whatever he would promise me, he would do.

The lawyer charged me a lot of money. He was one of a couple of people I had to be honest with and tell him the true story. I couldn't see any other way around it. However, since I spent so much money on this lawyer, that's why I felt so hurt and angry when the buyers of my house refused to pay the balance of 10,000 krons as they had promised on a hand shake. I will explain what happened. Unfortunately when the deadline came and I went to collect the money (we were leaving two days later), the buyer's wife said to me, "George, forget it. I am not going to pay you. You will never get the 10,000 krons. Good-bye." I was standing there feeling really, really angry and betrayed because 10,000 krons was a lot of money, but it was still nothing compared to what I had spent on the lawyer to protect them. If they would have known what I went through in order to save their house and not hurt them… they didn't care about me at all. It bothered me a lot, but it was water under the bridge, and I couldn't do anything about it.

This lawyer advised us about what needed to be done. He told me that we could not give our furniture and possessions away before we escaped. He said the house had to look like we were coming back from our "vacation." We had a very nice house. I had been working very hard and long hours overtime so I was making a fairly good living driving the truck and operating the crane. I also had a nice home because I knew how to get things done in this corrupted and messy society.

Helena and I immediately made a plan that we would replace nice and valuable things, saving them for our relatives, and substitute these with much cheaper items. For instance, we had a beautiful Czech-made crystal chandelier. We had a new color TV, that at that time, was not a common thing at all. So, of course, we took the chandelier down and replaced it with a light fixture with a paper shade. We replaced the color TV with a black and white one. We had to leave all the furniture. We boxed up the new bedding (replacing it with old) and a lot of clothes to eventually be given to Helena's mother. I had a lot of photography equipment that I wanted to pass on to my brother: cameras, an enlarger and other developing equipment.

So, guess who got involved now to help me stash my stuff – my lifelong friend, Simon, who I trusted the most. It was another big decision on my part to involve him with our secret. I approached him and told him the truth. I told him, "This is going to break your heart. It is breaking my heart. Sit down and take a deep breath. I have big news to tell you. We are going to escape. And I need your help stashing my stuff." This news hit him hard, but after he recovered from the shock, Simon's response was awesome. He said, "George, I guess you have been living half of your life under communism, so I am proud of you that you have enough guts to escape. You deserve to live the other half of your life in freedom. I'm happy for you that you are choosing the U.S. as your new home and I wish you lots of luck." I was relieved and impressed with his attitude. I explained to him that I needed to use his house to store the boxes we were giving to our relatives. We had to plan for the possibility of us being caught. In that case, the police would first look at Simon because they would find out really fast that he was my friend.

Transporting everything took some time because Simon lived 20 miles away on backcountry roads – no freeways or direct routes. We had to travel at night because that was the safest way to keep from being watched and being seen by neighbors. We buried everything under the coal in his basement including the box with all the pictures in this book. I put a sign on the box – "These pictures will not go to anybody. They are mine." The plan was that after the dust settled, Simon would distribute the labeled boxes to the various people. I left so much behind. The one thing I could not leave was the banjo my brother, Jaroslav, made for me. It was just too precious, too special. My brother made it for my 33rd birthday from scratch. I had a little dilemma of how to take this banjo with me, how to explain it at the border crossing. After all, we had a tent and were planning to camp, so I figured that a banjo was something that would fit with the story.

We had to be very careful what we packed for the "vacation." For instance, it was very important to take a Czech-English dictionary to use when we got to the U.S. because I couldn't speak English. To cover all of my bases in case the border guards would question me as to why I was carrying a Czech-English dictionary for a trip to Italy, I had to buy and pack a Czech-Italian dictionary as well.

Let's go back to the limousine driver, Josef, who hooked me up with the lawyer who guaranteed that the new owners of my house would never lose it... Well, this is getting very interesting. Josef was a driver for the son of the former communist president and had apparently gotten himself into circles of very powerful people. It turns out that he had been promoted to some important job and also had some influence at several checkpoints along the Iron Curtain. And because of this, he ended up being very instrumental in our escape. When I contacted him a second time, Josef told me that I could not have anything in our car – or on us – that would indicate that we were escaping and not coming back. He emphasized, "Everything must indicate that you are returning."

Now I have to explain another big obstacle – exchanging Czech currency to German marks or some other hard currency. I needed two different amounts of money, each for a different purpose. One amount would be money I exchanged on the black market and would be smuggled across the border to be used in those first few days in Austria and also to buy plane tickets to get to the U.S. I was very gullible and thought I could just buy plane tickets to the U.S., fly there and immediately be allowed to enter and stay. But that was another big obstacle that I will explain later. The other amount of money was needed for the "vacation" in Italy. And just to get that money from a Czech bank was a huge dilemma.

Along these lines, one of the signatures I had to get on the page 28 application was from the bank – to prove that we could be financially self-supporting in Italy. This was a vicious circle. They wouldn't give me the stamp and signature until I had the special extension – page 28! So this was a roadblock. This vicious circle was, in my opinion, designed by the government as a way to discourage anyone from traveling to any free country. As a result of this roadblock, I couldn't get the necessary signature for page 28 without having travel money and I couldn't get travel money without showing that I had page 28. It was a nightmare to get through all of this. The communists made this literally bulletproof! So I had to arm myself in order to also be bulletproof!

I went to the bank. Czech currency (krons) didn't have any value anywhere in the world. I had to have some hard currency – U.S. dollars, Austrians shillings, German marks, or Italian lire – or they would not allow me to go. The exchange rate was ridiculous. I had to take a lot of Czech money to turn into hard currency. So, I went to a very large, seven-story bank in downtown Prague and asked to exchange this money. And they said, "We don't have money for you," and in a polite but cold way, they let me know that I would never get it. I refused to take no for an answer and asked them again, "Please, there must be some way to help me." Their answer was repeated, "No!" So, I demanded to talk to the president of the bank. They told me I couldn't do this, and I said, "Yes I can. I am a very honest worker. My child is ill, and I WILL talk to anybody who is standing in my way. I must and I WILL protect the health of my child. I work hard enough and I've done everything right, and to protect the health of my child, I will talk to whomever is necessary – the president of your bank, or the president of the country." They stopped arguing with me and made me an appointment.

When I walked into the office of the bank president, he said, "What can I do for you? I heard you were quite determined to talk to me." I said, "I must go on vacation to Italy to save the health of my child. I am required to exchange this money." And he said, "We don't have enough money for everybody." I told him I didn't care how much money he would give me – that I just needed enough money to go to Italy for three weeks to protect the health of my child. He switched the subject, and we talked for a while about who I was – that I worked for a construction company, that I had been a truck driver and crane operator. I told him that I deserved this, that I had read so many articles in the newspaper saying that the government is looking out for us workers and that they are putting us first. I told him that I wanted him to take care of me, that I deserved it.

He said, "Well, I like you. I like your attitude and your determination, your experience. I am going to do two things for you. I just lost my chauffeur. I will give you the money, and when you come back from Italy, you will be my personal chauffeur." I was just staring at him in shock. I couldn't believe his proposal and that luck was finally on my side. The whole thing was to me, theatrical because I knew what I was after, but he didn't. So I started to play a game, and I asked how much he would pay me for my services. He said, "Don't worry about that. You won't complain. Just promise me when you come back you will be my personal chauffeur. I will arrange for the transfer from your company to me." I said, "I will do that. But we need to talk about some benefits." I knew I needed to look like I was coming back and that I was concerned about the job being good for me. So we made a deal about this job and then got back to the money exchange for the "vacation." He started to explain to me that he had only a small budget of hard currency so he would arrange for me to exchange a little bit less. He said, "I cannot give you enough money for three weeks – only enough for two weeks." At this point, I was thinking, "I don't care whether it is two or three weeks. I need to get out!" I stretched out my hand and asked, "Can we shake on this deal?" And he said, "Yes, you just go on vacation and when you come back, report here. You will be in good hands." We shook hands. Of course, I knew it was the last time that I would see him. I had my required money and signature for page 28. There were so many things that worked out... thinking back, it's almost unbelievable even very difficult things worked out, but it was not easy.

I want to go back to preparing for how to go through the border. Our car was full of stuff we needed for our "vacation" and also for survival during the first few days wherever we would end up. There were so many things we had to think through and go through. We had to get our birth certificates, my diploma, certificates of my education – things that I needed to apply for a job somewhere. I also had some black market money that I had exchanged on my own so I had something to start with. These things were very important to us, and we had to hide them and hide them well because if they would find these things at the border, that would have implicated us. It would have been proof of our escape plan.

You remember the former limousine driver, Josef, who had been promoted and now had a driver for himself. He told me, "George, I will try to help you at the border, but you cannot count on that because you never know what can happen. And also I might get a change in my work orders. You must make sure that you will go through even without me. So, all of your important papers must be hidden somewhere really well. The border crew is very strict and well trained. They know every single model of car in the world – every single hiding place. Expect that they will search you with your whole family and they will go entirely through your car. That is their job. Your papers must be hidden where no one can find them. So, be original and smart!"

I had big homework – to find, or create, some perfect hiding place. This might sound to you like a game, but it was not a game at all. It was extremely serious and dangerous. I was thinking constantly, for a couple of weeks at least, about some hidden place in our car that would never be discovered. I came up with an idea of an old wooden tool box that I had made and kept in the trunk of my car. It was full of tools, small old parts like nuts, bolts, fuses, light bulbs, spark plugs, etc. When I was looking at this box it looked perfect for the job because it was full of harmless little stuff that was kind of messy. I thought no one would take the time or have the desire to go through that mess. My handmade wooden toolbox was about twice the size of a photo album. It had a lid, and on the bottom of the box was a very thick (¾ inch) piece of felt to keep it from sliding around in the trunk. It had been in my car for a long time. It was dirty and had oil on it.

I emptied the toolbox, turned it upside down, and removed the dirty felt from the outside bottom of the box. Then I chiseled out a large cavity from the thick piece of wood that made up the bottom of the box. I put all of my documents and some money into a sealed plastic bag and inserted them into this cavity that I created. Finally I put a thin sheet of plywood over the bottom of the box, made it dirty, and nailed the dirty felt over everything. So, it was my old disgusting looking toolbox that, I felt, contained my whole life.

16

The Escape

The last couple of months I was counting each day, and I can't really say that I was happy or excited. I was actually more nervous, but I tried not to show it. Finally, the long time expected and hopefully well-planned day arrived, the day when we were going to escape. That was to be our D-Day. It was the end of May, 1980 and near the end of the school year.

I want to tell you that my last night in our home was kind of restless because I had millions of things on my mind. The word "home" had wider and wider meaning. It was not just the house; it was our homeland, the place of our birth, the place where we grew up, the place where we had our families, our friends, many fantastic memories, but unfortunately, also the place with a lot of big, very serious and unmanageable troubles. Now you might think that I am getting nostalgic, but I hope that you understand why. I think that if I wouldn't get nostalgic in a situation like this, there would have been something wrong with me. The communist regime was so deeply and strongly rooted in our country that everybody believed that communism would never ever go away. Not at least in our lifetime. So I knew that we were doing the right thing and not just for ourselves, but also FOR OUR CHILDREN! Now I had to stop thinking these thoughts and try to get some sleep because I really needed to be fresh and strong in the morning. I was finally able to get some sleep.

In the morning we woke up our kids a little bit earlier, so they got up just like usual. They thought they were going to school. (George, Jr. was nine, just finishing the third grade and Martin was seven, finishing first grade.) But then we finally told them, "No, you are not going to go to school. We are going on vacation! We are going to Italy so you can breathe fresh sea air and also just imagine! You are going to be swimming in the sea!" We had to wait until the last minute to tell them so they would not be able to talk with any other little kids in school or in the neighborhood. We also had to tell them enough so they could answer some potential questions that they might be asked by the border guards. We had to make them believe we were on our way to Italy for vacation. They didn't know how far away it was, but they were very excited about swimming in the big waves in the sea. Remember, Czechoslovakia isn't connected to any shoreline with a sea or an ocean. Every kid had a dream to swim in or at least see the ocean. Helena and I had never seen any sea either. It was very exotic for all of us to be able to see the sea, kind of like somebody who lives in the tropics and sees snow for the first time.

We had loaded up the car the night before. I had practiced loading the car many nights prior to this final loading. I want to tell you, when we got into the car, my nostalgic thoughts were back again. I knew this was the last time that we would see the house that we spent so much time building. I knew I couldn't involve myself too much with these thoughts because I would never get anywhere. I had to stay strong and play "cool" in front of Helena and the kids. I started to drive southeast toward the border with Austria. The excitement was really, really high. The kids were so excited because they were going to the sea to swim in salt water.

We got out of the Prague area and we were zooming south to the border. It was in the morning. I had a rendezvous with Josef – the one who hooked me up with the lawyer and who had some influence at the border. This rendezvous was planned for the last town before the border crossing, Znojmo, at an exact time, 11:00 in the morning. I also had something else I had to do in this town.

I had the keys for our house that we had sold and did not own anymore – but where we had been living on borrowed time for a couple of weeks. I was sending one key to the people who bought the house and the other key to the lawyer that Josef had hooked me up with. This lawyer wanted to make sure that everything in the house was in the right order and he needed access to the house to be sure it looked right. I didn't care at that time if this guy would steal something from our house. I could not have cared less. I had to mail these keys from the post office in Znojmo, the last town before crossing the border.

This rendezvous worked just like clockwork. Josef was there and had told his chauffeur to stop so he could take a break, stretch and take a walk. He needed to get away from the car so the chauffeur would not see us meeting him and suspect something. We met in front of the post office, where Josef told me his plan. He said, "George, let me drive there first. I will do some work there, and when you show up, I will try to disrupt the border crossing procedure. Just be there in the next half hour. I wish you luck..."

My heart was pounding. This year and a half of preparation was getting to the finish line. I knew that all this endless preparation of our plot, going through so many difficult times and details, was getting to the end. I was only a few kilometers and minutes from this finish line. I prayed with my heart pounding harder and harder, that we were going to be able to get through the Iron Curtain safely without being caught, that we would soon get to the free side of the world. It was very emotional for me – and for Helena as well. We were petrified and we still had to play "cool" – it was very important not to show any emotions. This was a big test to see how much of an emotional load a human could take. The kids were excited because they still thought it was just a vacation.

I waited for half an hour, took a deep breath and started to drive toward the border. We drove through all the check points, showing our passports and that all important "sacred and holy Special Page 28!" Finally we got to the border, and they opened the gate before the Iron Curtain – like the one I was explaining to you earlier, the one with the big iron beam. Remember, this was not the same gate as the one I was observing from my crane. That one was on the German border. This border was with Austria on the south. But it was basically the same thing.

We were finally at the Iron Curtain. Immediately we were surrounded by the border officers and soldiers. They started their routine – what they did to everybody. They demanded to see our documents again. They asked a lot of questions about where we were going – for how long. They told us to get out of the car. They opened the trunk. They opened the hood. They started to unload everything and inspect. I was just like a little puppet. I was listening to all these commands. I was excited and scared at the same time. The guards were very nosy, efficient, official and strict. They were going through everything. I was glancing from time to time at my toolbox with its secret pocket. Every time they touched it, my heart stopped. My job was to play "cool." I was also watching how Helena and the kids were reacting, and to be prepared to jump into any conversation in case even one word from them would endanger our plan. I had to create the impression that I was an honest and innocent citizen with nothing to hide and nothing to lie about. But I also knew I was up against well-trained and sneaky border guards.

And then, all of a sudden, in the middle of everything, when they were going through all our stuff, Josef showed up. He just sort of leisurely walked up and started talking to the duty officer, the guy in charge of this shift. This duty officer had a number of officers, or agents, under his command. They did not have uniforms like I had ever seen before. They were in black jumpsuits with all their gear attached – ready to shoot. Josef was telling something to the shift officer. I really didn't know how much power Josef had. I remember the shift officer looked at Josef, and Josef was making a face like, "Well, I just told you..." It was as if Josef were giving him some kind of command, telling him it was not necessary to take the whole car apart, that this was just an innocent family with little kids and you didn't have to be so brutal. I heard him say, " I need to talk to you and show you something back in the office." He then gave the officer a firm command, "Just finish this! I don't have that much time. I'm on a schedule." It was part of Josef's plan. It was obvious to me. I knew it, and Josef knew it. But nobody else knew it. However, three or four soldiers were excited about turning everything upside down in our car. Josef had to tell them, "It's OK, guys. That is enough. Stop and put everything back together." Finally the shift officer called off the guards and said, "Yeah, we have to go and do something else right now." The duty officer gave me my papers back and said, "Everything is fine." Josef stayed for a few seconds. He gave me a look and kind of blinked his eyes. As he was leaving he looked over his shoulder and whispered, "Good luck." This is just all coming back and very much real...and extremely emotional for me to relive this. I'm sorry – please give me a couple of minutes...

We just put everything back together and closed the trunk. We had been practicing and practicing how to pack everything. So, I knew where everything went. I was very fast. I closed the trunk and the hood. I got in the car and drove through the Iron Curtain. It was the first time in my 36 years...

I was on the other side of the border...

I cannot continue right now...I'm so emotional again...

When we were far enough away from the border that nobody could hear me, I started to scream. My wife started to cry. The kids were totally confused. Then we changed our role. She started to scream, and I started to cry. The kids still didn't know what was going on. They were totally puzzled, looking at each other and trying to figure out what was happening. They were too young, too innocent, naïve and gullible. Then something very strange happened. Something big. I had to pull over on the shoulder and stop the car. I felt unbelievably relieved and started to realize our dream had become reality – **WE WERE FREE!!** I don't know how to describe this beautiful and warm feeling of happiness. It was better than if someone would tell you that you had won $100 million. We had made it to Austria, a free county!! We had made it to freedom. **WE WERE FREE!!!**

After I put myself back together to be able to drive, I got on the road again. At the first stop, I needed to get directions to Vienna. I had gotten a name from Jaroslav (my former partner on the crane) of a couple who had escaped in 1968 to Vienna. But contact with them was never arranged. They had no idea I was coming or who I was. I hoped that they would be our first helpful contact. I had an address and a name but that was all. I also needed to ask where I could exchange some of my money for Austrian schillings. Trying to read the German road signs was impossible. (Austria is a German speaking country.) Remember, I had studied Russian under communism for 14 years. We had been told and taught that Russian was the world's language – that everyone spoke Russian because Russia was so powerful. I didn't believe them 100%, but I still thought that with my Russian I could get by. So, I stopped and asked two Austrians in Russian where to go to exchange money. They looked at me like I was from Mars. I started to ask very slowly – first in Russian, then in Czech. They were just shaking their heads. Then they said, "Do you speak English?" I knew two words – "hello" and "thank you." So, we were kind of drawing pictures on the ground to figure out what I needed to know.

17

A Bitter Realization – and a Final Decision

We did get to Vienna that day. When we finally found the street and building of our hopefully first contact, it was very late at night. We didn't want to ring the bell on some stranger's door this late who we had never met. But we did need some help. So, we parked on the street in front of their apartment building to sleep in the car overnight. It was very uncomfortable since the car was kind of small and really packed. We were exhausted, and on top of that, we had to sleep in a sitting position. We were thirsty and hungry. We were partially happy, partially confused, and partially still scared. The boys still didn't know what was going on and because of their age, they thought this was the way we would go to get to Italy. We were waiting until morning to be polite before knocking on the door.

The next morning, we rang the doorbell on the panel next to the main entrance door of the apartment building. The person answered through the speaker phone. I started to speak Czech and the person answered in Czech. They were Czech people, immigrants from 1968. I introduced myself. The guy's name was Vasek Schuster. He came down from his apartment, and saw that I had two sleeping young boys in the car, a tired wife, and that I was also very tired. I told him, "I just escaped from Czechoslovakia."

I'm sorry, I can't go on right now. Again, this is so emotional for me, remembering how all this happened. Please give me a minute...

Anyway, Vasek's eyes lit up and he smiled and said, "Congratulations!" After a few seconds of silence, he asked, "What are your plans?" I said, "I want to go to the United States. I need to get plane tickets." He smiled and said, "Mister, it does not work this way."

Then he invited us into his apartment and offered us the use of the bathroom to refresh ourselves. In the meantime he made tea to serve with a light breakfast. The boys were still tired but they soon were occupied with exploring some toys they found in the apartment. They were not at all interested in the adult conversation taking place. When we sat down and made ourselves comfortable, he explained, "You are on the free side of the world. You can do anything you want, but you cannot go to the United States without the United States approving you first. You can buy tickets, but you cannot step a foot on their soil. They will send you back to where you came from – to Vienna." We were shocked to hear this. I asked, "What do I have to do?" He said, "You have to go to the camp for refugees. You have to turn yourselves in to the Austrian authorities, ask for political asylum and go into the camp for refugees. Hopefully you will be admitted but, I'm telling you, it is like being in jail!"

My head was spinning. This was too much negative information. I didn't know what we were getting into and even if I followed his advice, I had no idea how long we would have to stay in this refugee camp. A month or two, a year? There was no agency in communist Czechoslovakia where I could get a brochure on how to escape or how to start and overcome difficulties in a new FREE country. I was completely and totally unprepared for this new information.

So there I was – a civilized person, dressed kind of decent – prepared to get on a boat or on a plane to the U.S., and I am finding out that the gate to the U.S. is closed to us – that we cannot do it. So, I spent quite a bit of time with Vasek. He was telling me very good information, but I was so unhappy to hear these facts. I was just crushed. I was more scared than any other time because we had burned all of our bridges in Czechoslovakia. We had sold the house. At that moment, with all the turmoil and confusion going on in my head, I have to admit that I started to consider going back to Czechoslovakia. I couldn't believe that I was actually thinking about doing that, but I was calculating that it would have still been legal to return. But what kind of option would that have been? The communist police would love to have me back and continue to watch me. Sooner or later they would come up with some reason to arrest me and put me away for a long, long time. And on the other hand, I wasn't single – I felt that it was my duty to protect my family. This was way too serious to gamble. I could go to Italy for two weeks and go back to Czechoslovakia. I could have gone back, but that would have been a total disaster. There were people working on my plot, trying to cover my escape. I had made agreements with this lawyer. It would have been so disastrous for Helena's family and for my family. We built the house from absolute scratch and worked on it so hard and for so long. And we had sold it secretly. We had used the money to get out.

So, to go back??? How? Why? What to do? It was literally too much for me. Helena was always an excellent person in difficult times. She was very supportive and just let me work out what to do. Finally I made the decision to buy us some time, so I told Vasek, "I am so disappointed and confused. I have to sort it out. We are going to Italy and go on our vacation. I have money for it. I am going to go to Italy and think this through and sleep on it and get some good rest."

Vasek understood. He was very supportive and he was wishing us luck. He had a family – a wife and little girl, maybe six or seven. His wife was a nurse in a hospital, his daughter was in school and we didn't have a chance to meet them. They had left their home early in the morning before we could politely knock on their door. Vasek gave us his phone number, and he said, "Whatever you will decide, you are a friend of mine." He had been through something similar 12 years before, but nothing this drastic. It had been so much easier to get out then. 1968 was the year when the communists opened the borders (Iron Curtain) for a relatively short time to get rid of the "rebels." He didn't have a family then and he was not leaving Europe. He also settled in a neighboring country. In 1980 it was totally different. I wanted to go as far away as possible on this planet, to the

Vasek Schuster, my new friend in Vienna

other side of the world, with a wife and two small children. When we were leaving his apartment, he shook my hand and said, "Whatever you decide, if you will need me, I will help you." What a guy!

I want to apologize for being so emotional from time to time, but I am telling you this story in such detail that I am reliving this all over again. I hope that you understand all the problems and the important life-changing decisions that I was making under very difficult circumstances.

At about rush hour, we set out for Italy. It was the first time in 36 years of my life to drive on a freeway. There was only one freeway in all of Czechoslovakia at that time. It was only 20 km long and still partially under construction. I was driving south out of Vienna in heavy traffic on the freeway, and my mind was so overwhelmed with so much bad news from

Vasek's apartment. I couldn't concentrate. I needed to stop to get a little break, get into the fresh air and recuperate a little bit so I could function again. There was an exit and I remember that the exit was under construction, blocked with cones and barricades. I saw this as my chance to pull off. I put my right blinker on. I got off and got behind those cones. I stopped our car and went out. I was just breathing hard. Helena also got out and said, "Well, what are you going to do?" I said, "We don't have that many options. We are totally screwed." Everything was collapsing. All the excitement, all that getting to the finish line, reaching our goal – all of it was now collapsing big time. There was nothing to hold on to. I felt so overwhelmed – we were just drowning. Helena was very supportive again. She trusted me. She believed I was capable of fixing things up and building ourselves back up from nothing. She just said, "Do whatever you think is best." I said, "I think it is really best to just get to Italy and see how I feel tomorrow, the next day or one week from now. I have to sleep on this. I really and literally must sleep on this." It was just too much in the last 30 hours. At this point, the kids started asking questions about why we stopped on the freeway and wanted to know what were we talking about. We didn't know what to tell them because we didn't know ourselves. We kept coming up with excuses, pretending that everything was just fine.

After a little bit of rest, we got back into the car and continued driving in the direction of Italy. We drove all night and stopped in Venice the next day. I was totally exhausted, physically and emotionally. The last 48 hours I had slept only four hours, very uncomfortably, in a crowded car in Vienna, and what was on my mind was indescribable – should we go back, should we not, what should we do?

You probably wonder if I know of anybody who crossed the through the Iron Curtain and then returned to Czechoslovakia. I knew of a number of people who returned after getting out, but none of them returned after having escaped. These people, as I mentioned earlier, were movie stars, singers, athletes, scientists, etc. Over the years, a few of them defected. You might remember some of the names – figure skater Hana Maskova (USA), tennis player Martina Navratilova (USA), the hockey players Stastnys (Canada – no relation)...

I also knew myself one person who left and then came back. It was my good friend Louie. I will explain what and how it happened to the best of my knowledge. Louie and I never talked about his escape before it happened.

You just didn't talk about that even with your best friend. However, if it were absolutely necessary, then you would have to. But knowing Louie so well, I knew that this was on his mind for many years. In my very private and personal opinion, it was just a question of when he would escape.

Louie had studied the English language since he was a little boy. His parents paid for private lessons. He also had studied a lot of things about America because he was very interested in that subject. By the way, I want to brag about Louie's talent for languages. By the time he was an adult, he was fluent in three languages – Czech, English and Russian. And he could also get by in German.

This is what I know. It was 1966, before the Russians put the boot on us. Louie signed up with a very wealthy person in London who was building an amphitheatre. This man wanted to do something nice for young people from all over the world. He advertised that anybody from anywhere in the world, including communist countries, could come and help to build this amphitheatre. I need to explain something. Communists didn't like any free country, and were always talking about them very negatively. But on the other hand, they loved to talk – and very loudly – about the friendship of workers around the world. They loved the terminology like "international work force," "friendship of youth from all over the world." They were making posters where workers and young people of all races were raising red flags in front of crowds and looking very happy. That was all communist propaganda, that people around the world are so eager to carry red flags.

Therefore communists didn't mind to send one or two young people to London to participate in the amphitheatre project. If that theater had been built in Warsaw, Poland, or in Moscow, Russia, they would have probably sent at least 1,000 young people there. Louie signed up for this job, and he hit the jackpot. He really lucked out. He was chosen. He went to London to build this theater, and he met so many people from many other free countries. He met this young guy from West Germany named Hans, and they became good friends. Then Louie really surprised me. He came back from England. I was not expecting him to ever come back. I was just thinking, "Louie is gone forever because once you get out from behind the Iron Curtain, you don't come back!" But when he came back, he didn't share much. He was very reserved talking about what he saw, what he was thinking, and to be really honest, I didn't see him much. I knew, though, that Louie was cooking up some secret plan for escaping again. I don't want to sound like 1966 was easy to get through the Iron Curtain. Not at all. But, what was a big thing on Louie's side was that he was single and then he proved to the authorities that they could trust him because he came back from his previous trip to England. So I didn't ask any questions and I gave him lots of space. I had plenty of things to take care of for my upcoming wedding.

I also need to explain that after Louie and I came back from the military, our childhood and youth was over. We became adults with our own ideas of how, where and with whom we will live. We were still best friends, but we didn't have that much time anymore to see each other like when we were kids. We still did some things together – camping, hiking, biking, and volleyball – but it wasn't every day like we used to do. I had found a girlfriend (Helena) and I was getting ready to marry. The wedding took place, and Louie was my best man and very shortly afterward, he totally disappeared. I later figured out that one of the reasons why he came back was to be my best man at our wedding. The second time when he crossed the border, he knew just what to do, and he was gone!

When I was making my own escape plans, I had to rely on someone who was trustworthy, my friend and first crane partner, Jaroslav Zeman. He always felt that he owed me a big favor because I helped him a great deal once when he was injured on a construction job. I mentioned a little bit about him already. I will explain what happened.

We were assigned to a job site when the injury occurred involving his foot. We were working with a bunch of granite blocks to make a curb on the sidewalk, and we needed to move these blocks a short distance. It was a common practice to tie (to "choke") these large stones into a big bundle with a heavy steel cable, hang them on the hook and then move the crane. Jaroslav was walking next to the crane beside the load of granite blocks. I was driving the crane very carefully. No one was in the cab working the tower that was locked into a certain position. It was kind of bumpy because the road was under construction. I was driving this mobile crane very slowly. Even so, the load started to swing a bit. Jaroslav was walking right next to the crane and tried to stop the load from swinging. Unfortunately, he was in a bad spot because, all of a sudden, the steel cable broke. These 800-1,000 pound granite blocks were flying. He jumped, but one big granite block landed on his foot. It was an extremely serious and bad injury.

We were very close to the medical clinic and I immediately took him to the doctor. I started to pound on the door very aggressively and said very strictly that it was an emergency and that we needed immediate help. The doctor took off Jaroslav's boot. The injury was very ugly and the doctor said it was too serious. He said he was not qualified to do this complicated surgery and especially in his clinic office. Jaroslav needed to be transferred to a good hospital with some skilled surgeons. I asked this doctor to call the ambulance and have Jaroslav taken to the hospital. The doctor and his nurse really tried to make an arrangement but it wasn't working in that rotten and corrupt system. So I immediately took over. I grabbed the phone (remember it was way before the time of cellular phones and the number "911" didn't exist) and called a very good friend of mine who was the head nurse in one of the largest hospitals in Prague. The name of the hospital was Bulovka and my friend was Jana. Unfortunately I couldn't get through since all the lines in the hospital were busy.

Jaroslav was in excruciating pain and bleeding heavily. I needed to act quickly. So I called Jana's husband Honza (in English "Jack") with whom I used to work in the electronic factory. Jana and Honza were very good family friends of ours. Luckily I got through to Honza and told him that we had a serious job accident with the crane involving my partner. I explained that this was an emergency and I couldn't get through to the hospital. So I needed him to keep calling his wife Jana to get a good orthopedic surgeon ready and be watching for us because we were coming. In the meantime, the ambulance finally arrived so I felt lucky, but the ambulance driver said he wasn't supposed to take any injury cases to Bulovka Hospital because it was Wednesday and on Wednesdays they were doing only scheduled in-patient surgeries. I explained to the driver that he must ignore this Wednesday policy and take us to this hospital and nowhere else because I had already made arrangements. So he did exactly that.

We were zooming through heavy traffic through Prague with emergency lights and sirens on to "our" hospital. Honza luckily had gotten a hold of Jana in the meantime, and she was waiting for us with her friend, a good orthopedic surgeon. After all, it worked like clockwork, but you always needed to know someone who knew someone and basically do all arrangements yourself. What an advantage to have "free" medical!! If we had waited on this socialistic way of doing things, Jaroslav could have bled to death.

So this was how I helped to save Jaroslav's foot. Actually part of his toes needed to be amputated, but he could still walk and run normally, and you wouldn't know that he had had such a horrible injury. And yes, Jaroslav did later repay the favor when I really needed him. He was the one who hooked me up with the people who took me to the woods for that one signature. He was also the one who gave me the address of Vasek in Vienna. At that time, Jaroslav was not sure if that contact was going to work, but after all, it did.

I need to go back to my story of how we were getting to Italy. But first, I would like to mention a new experience for me that happened on our way. It was a long drive through the night. We were all tired and so thirsty. I had some German marks, and I thought I could buy some drinks for us. The stores were closed because it was the middle of the night. I spotted an open bar so I stopped in front of it. Oh my, we were so thirsty. Of course, I wanted to buy a lot to drink for everybody. Helena gave me all the empty containers we had, two 2-liter bottles and some plastic cups. She asked me to fill them all with Coca-Cola. I thought I had plenty of money to fill them up since I had this German change in my pocket. I walked into the bar, and with hand language, I asked for Coca-Cola. The bartender and the people around him didn't understand my "language," but they understood that I wanted Coca-Cola. I was thinking I was so rich with my German marks in my hand that I could buy plenty of Coke to fill all my containers. So, I held out my change. The bartender looked at that and gave me a very small cup of Coke. I was shocked! There were other people in the bar who were watching, so I knew I was not being cheated. I actually became the center of attention. But that one cup of Coca-Cola cost what seemed like a lot of money. I was thinking immediately how much this cup would cost in Czech krons. I knew how many Czech krons I had to exchange for the German marks in my hand. It was like two hours of wages. It was absolutely unreal. I asked if I could get water for the rest of the containers. The kids were waiting. They were so thirsty and each got a couple of swallows of Coke, but that was OK, they were happy anyway. The water satisfied their thirst.

The point of this episode is that I knew immediately that I wasn't as rich as I thought, that the German marks that I exchanged on the black market for a lot of Czech krons would not get us very far. Czech krons that I had to work very hard for had very little value in the free world.

The next day we arrived in Venice. It was pouring down rain. It was horrible. We didn't have enough money for a hotel, but we had a tent. The kids had been asking for more than 48 hours, "Are we there, yet? Where is the sea? Where is the ocean?" They had no idea why we had stopped in Vienna and spent so much time there. They were trying very hard to be patient. They still thought we were on vacation because we hadn't told them what exactly was going on. We were trying to find some area in Venice to pitch the tent – somewhere not very populated, somewhere out of sight, maybe somewhere on the outskirts of the city. I was driving around and we couldn't find anything suitable anywhere. Then we got to a less populated place that looked like a spot teenagers would use at night for drinking and partying. It was very messy. There were broken bottles and a small fire pit. We started to clean up this place because we were afraid we wouldn't find anything better and we were losing daylight. In the meantime, we were getting hungry and I knew that with our very limited budget, we couldn't go to any restaurant, but we were fine in that we had some leftovers of sandwiches and crackers. It was very bleak, a very bad situation. Very uncomfortable. Very tough. We worked there for about an hour, trying to make some sort of camp out of this messy area. We knew we were in much trouble. All of us were wet, hungry, thirsty, tired and I was still dealing with the uncertainty of our future. On top of everything else, we didn't speak the language and couldn't talk to anyone. I hoped that the next day would be better, but for now we just wanted to set up the tent in a reasonable spot and get some sleep. We started to piggle and figgle (my way of describing "messing" with things!) with our tent.

I guess I am a little bit of a romantic and therefore, in hard and bad times, I start to dream kind of sarcastically. At that moment, I started to dream that somebody would come, tap on my shoulder and say, "Hey, come to my house. Have a drink. Dry your feet. Get some sleep, etc." Well, guess what? The unbelievable started to happen. There were a couple of houses nearby with barred windows. It was obvious that crime was a very common thing there. All of a sudden, a door to one of these houses opened, and two young girls, maybe 12 or 13 years old, walked out to us. They started to talk to us in Italian, but we didn't understand a word. They were trying by sign language to tell us that we were welcome to come into their house. The door was open, and there was an old grandmother standing in the doorway, motioning for us to come on in. I realized that they must have watched us for a while from their house. At first we were a little bit shy, but we didn't hesitate for too long and we went in, not knowing what to expect. We hoped for some warm tea, but maybe she just wanted to ask what we were doing there. So, with a Czech-English dictionary, their little bit of knowledge of English, and lots of hand language, we were able to communicate that we were Czechs in Italy on vacation. We said that we wanted to camp overnight. They insisted we bring our sleeping bags in and sleep inside on the floor. It was very nice, something that we really needed. We needed to be under a roof, not worrying about anything for at least a moment. The kids were playing with the two girls and they became instant friends. The whole episode – with this old lady and the two girls – was just like something you would read in some naïve fairy tale. But it happened and it was just like a little bandage on my wound. We really appreciated their hospitality! In the morning they were waving and telling us goodbye. We were so thankful. We did not tell them that we had escaped. We had only told Vasek in Vienna. I would not have told even someone who spoke Czech. It was far too complicated to tell someone who didn't speak our language. Besides, I was still very cautious about talking to anyone about our secret plot. I worried about our safety. I mean politically. That was the way we had lived. It took a long, long time before I got used to talking to strangers freely.

The next day, since we were in Venice, we visited some historical sights. It was exciting but it was exciting in a different way for me. Remember, I was born and grew up in Prague, a city that many people feel is the most beautiful city in the world. I also had helped to restore some historical sites there. It was a pleasure and wonderful experience looking at the beauty of Venice and admiring the talent of some great Italian artists. Michelangelo was always one of my favorites.

But now back to our travels. Close to evening, we finally got to the Adriatic Sea and found a campground. The kids were so excited. It felt almost impossible for them and for us as well, to see a real sea! I had promised them that that day they would be swimming in the sea. I had told them that even if it were raining, or even if the sea would be frozen – I would hammer a hole in it – that day they would be swimming in the sea. Because we were running out of daylight, we had to at least pitch the tent. And then, of course, since I had promised, I went to swim with them. We thought it was really awesome. But this was nothing compared to the next day. The next day was absolutely beautiful!

We were very happy. The boys were starting to make friends with other kids in the campground. Everyone was from different countries and it was very interesting to see how well the children got along with each other even though they didn't speak the same language. Their parents were looking at us and each other, smiling, and in their faces, I read that we were welcome. It was a pleasant feeling and also very important to us. Some were speaking German, some were speaking Swedish. We were in a totally different world. Some people from as far away as Canada were also camping there. And there were even some Czech people, maybe some long time immigrants. Of course, we didn't tell them anything about our plans, but at least we had someone to say hello to in Czech. We had roughly ten days in front of us where the kids could play and "breathe the warm sea air." I had a big decision to make, but first I needed a good rest to regenerate and recuperate mentally and physically.

It took about three days for me to get over the huge stress and shocks that had hit me in the last few days. I found myself relaxing, and I also started to think a little bit differently about spending our money. I recalculated and even though prices were very expensive for us, we could still buy some normal meals, fresh fruit, and ice cream for the kids.

Our boys enjoying a display of fresh fruit in Italy.

Remembering how much it cost to buy the Coca-Cola on the trip, I was very interested to know how much it would cost to live in the free world. The other families were buying ice cream and hot dogs, and all kinds of good dinners and bottles of wine. In the campground it seemed like everyone had a bottle of wine. There was no way I was going to use my money for wine. I had to save it for something more important. I was looking at this lifestyle – at this relaxed society. I also knew that people had their jobs, and most likely, they worked hard. Therefore they made enough to be able to afford their vacations. I knew how to work and enjoyed working and working hard so I would be able to provide for my family like I always had. The only difference now was I wouldn't be paid in Czech krons. Well, that was a no brainer... that sure sounded good to me! It took me about three days to take it all in. And I said to myself, "I think I like where I am. I like the people and their attitudes. They are happy and friendly to each other. We are strangers to them and they don't need us. Yet, they are nice to us." We couldn't communicate, but there was always some other way to make ourselves understood. I was really starting to like it. I remember how hard I was thinking about what we should do, what would be the best decision to make for our future. I felt that my decision was going be a tremendously responsible step. Over the next four days, all my terrible worries started to melt and I was able to make the decision, and I remember that moment very well.

Having a great time in the Adriatic Sea surf in Italy.

The kids were happily playing on the shore, and I was lying on the beach watching them. I was looking at these people from many different countries, being happy and having fun, and I was thinking, "I am sure that they didn't have to have some 20 stupid signatures to come here. They didn't have to lower themselves to ask some non-educated moron with a communist pin for permission. They certainly didn't have to sell their homes to be able to bribe under the table some greedy, dishonest and powerful corrupt authorities. Most likely these vacationers made their own decision where, when, with whom and for how long they will come. And that's why they were here and were so relaxed."

Well, that was the life I wanted for my family and myself. I want to admit that these thoughts greatly and positively influenced me. I was still watching our kids. Then I looked at my wife and I told her, "Helena, I just made the decision. We are not going back to Czechoslovakia. We are going back to Vienna. We will go to Vasek and ask him to direct us to the camp for refugees. We have gone through so much, and this camp and many other immigration obstacles will be nothing compared to what we have been through already. Let's just finish this. I want us to live freely like these people around us. I want to live in the United States and be free! I want to start our new life there. And that's what we need to focus on. That is where I am turning my course from now on and nothing will stop me! I am not scared anymore. Everything is going to be fine." And that is exactly what I started to work on.

18

Life in Austria: The Camp for Refugees

After our shortened vacation in Italy, we went back to Vienna and knocked on Vasek's door. It was in the afternoon, and I remember his wife was on her way home from work. He was glad we had come back, offered that we could stay with them for the night and the next day we would start to take some legal steps. And we did. He took me to an office in downtown that looked like the United Nations. It was a very tall and beautiful white building, and we talked to some kind of American representatives. It was not the U.S. Embassy. I was in the U.S. Embassy in Vienna much later. Vasek was trying to explain our situation, to get me some kind of green light for us to go to the United States. But everybody was saying, "No, no, no. He is not going to the United States. He has to go to the camp for refugees. We will not let anybody go to the United States without going through the legal system. He has to apply for entering the United States and be approved. If he is going to go there without legal permission, he will be turned back."

The camp for refugees was about 25 km south of Vienna in the little town of Traiskirchen. We had to go into this camp. That day, we turned ourselves over to the Austrian police and asked for political asylum. Even though I wanted to ask for political asylum from the United States, I had to follow the legal procedure that required me to ask for asylum from the first free country I put my foot on. If we were approved by the Austrians, only then could I ask for the same from the U.S. This is a story by itself, but I will get into that later.

We checked ourselves into this camp for refugees. And I tell you, it was like a jail, at least at first. They stripped us of everything. We gave up our passports, our car, all our belongings, everything, ending up with only the clothes on our backs. We were just like prisoners. Our whole family stayed together in one cell equipped with really old metal bunk beds. They fed us with horrible food. This was a large, old barracks that had been converted into this jail. There were bars on the doors and the windows. It looked, felt and sounded like Alcatraz. When the bars on the doors slammed shut, the sound was very scary and echoed through the long, cold and empty hallways. It was very spooky. I don't want to sound like I'm complaining about this place. I understood why we were there. I'm just trying to explain exactly how it was. We were scared and very uncomfortable. But we had chosen to go this route, and we had to prepare ourselves to go through some really, really difficult and lengthy times. We hoped that this would pay off and at the end, we would be allowed to immigrate to the United States. At that time we didn't know much, we didn't know how long we would have to stay in this "jail," but they were preparing us for staying there for a long time.

I remember the bathrooms looked so bad. The floor was flooded two inches with urine. When the kids needed to go to the bathroom, I would have to hold them above the toilet and then I would tell them, "Now you can pee. Hurry up and pee!" Then I would carry them back, and I would wash my feet and my shoes. It was very, very primitive and nasty. We were given old, holey military blankets – very itchy. They gave us a spoon, a metal cup and a metal dish with a handle on it. Everything was very beaten up. The smell from the kitchen was really, really bad, but we ate the food anyway. What a "lovely" environment! We were not allowed to go outside and were behind bars the whole time. I knew that this was the procedure that everyone must go through.

These first days, we had to stay in these cells that were called "isolation." We didn't know how long we would have to be there. We were prepared maybe for two weeks or a month. Anything longer than that sounded very scary. Now, can you imagine how difficult it was to explain to our children why we were in this jail-like situation! It was not easy to come up with some realistic reasons that a seven and nine-year-old would buy. We had to assure them very frequently that everything was going to be all right. We were explaining that we were in a foreign country, and they have different and strict policies and different ways of doing things. We tried very hard to stay calm and not to show in front of the kids that we worried or to give them any indication by our actions that they needed to be concerned. Every time they asked or expressed some doubts, we assured them that they were safe and everything was going to be all right soon. I think we became such good actors that we could have been nominated in Hollywood for an Oscar! I wish that we could have told our boys the truth that our intention was to go to the U.S. However, this would not have been a good time or place to add another burden on their shoulders, for them to realize they would never be going home again. Also, we couldn't tell them at that time because we didn't know ourselves what was going to happen, where we would end up. We knew that this would be a very lengthy process, and we didn't know if political asylum would be granted to us, if we would be allowed to go to the U.S.

After a couple of weeks in this situation, some guards came and were barking out orders in German, telling us to get out of the cell. It was like in the movies about the concentration camps of WWII. So we got out and we were shocked, but this time pleasantly. There was a beautiful coach bus sitting there in front of the building. They gave me back the keys and papers for my car, and they said, "Your family will be on the bus and you are to follow this bus in your car." This all felt like a miracle. I had my car back, but not for long. We had no idea where they were going to take us. I hoped that whatever was going to happen would turn out better than the "isolation jail."

They loaded a number of families, ours included, into this bus, and we drove maybe another 30 km southwest. We came to a beautiful little town – Neuhaus was the name – and there was a big four-story old hotel-like building. This building was already occupied by various refugees, most of them single people. There were some vacant rooms on the third and fourth floors. Our family ended up on the fourth floor. These rooms didn't have any furniture except two old single beds with old stained mattresses and no bedding. It was fine with us since we had gotten our car back and had all sorts of things in the trunk for camping, including our sleeping bags. We furnished our room the best we could and always kept it clean. We even spruced it up with wildflowers from a nearby meadow, keeping them in a large pickle jar.

This "hotel" looked nice, but only from the outside. Inside it looked like a barracks, with one bathroom (toilet only) for each floor. There was no shower in the whole building, only one bathtub. Each floor had a washroom with a long metal trough with a number of faucets above it. We used this for any water needs – drinking, hand washing, shaving, tooth brushing, washing dishes and laundry. They started to treat us like refugees. There was nothing wrong with that. We were refugees. Actually I was very happy – it was 100% better than isolation at the refugee camp in Traiskirchen. They fed us. The food, to me, was decent but many people were complaining. They said, "We cannot eat this." I asked them, "Well, how much did you pay for it?" We were on the shoulders of the Austrian government. I think they took good care of us. They didn't have to – they didn't have to do anything. They could have said, "Get out of here." But they didn't. Lots of people were complaining, saying, "This food looks spoiled. It's getting green!" I always argued with them, "It looks fine to me. What do you want? You are the problem, and you will be a bigger problem if you are going to continue to complain." I really did appreciate what Austria did for us. In fact, the Austrian government was awarded the Humanitarian Nobel prize for taking care of so many refugees.

We were very lucky to be able to get into this big old hotel. The reason was that the main refugee camp in Traiskirchen was full so they made good use of this old building. We were still registered in the main camp, but we were like a little branch of the main camp. We were chosen for Neuhaus because priority was given to people with families to get them out of the ugly main camp.

The old hotel filled up pretty quickly. There were people from Albania, Poland, Ukraine, people from all over the world. Many came from poor and developing countries that had never seen a flushing toilet before. Every time we went to the bathroom, there was some poop or pee on the floor. We knew who was doing that because if you went in after somebody, you would get an idea. So, we people from civilized countries were standing guard, and we were teaching people how to use the toilet seat, how to flush, and how to wash their hands after each use. They were looking at us as if to say, "I have never done it this way." And we would say, "Well, that is the way you are going to do it here." They were really, really poor and primitive in some ways. We were trying to civilize them a little bit, so we shared with them some of our extras, including toys for their kids. They were appreciative and they were cooperating.

We were free to go almost anywhere we wanted. I mean walk anywhere, because even though we had gotten our car back, we couldn't drive it. It would have been illegal since getting car insurance in Austria was very complicated and expensive. We walked and also hitchhiked a lot. Hitchhiking was very easy – there was almost no way a car with an empty seat would go by without stopping for you. I felt very good about that because when I was a teenager, I was hitchhiking a lot because I didn't have a car. It was a way for young people to get around on their trips in our country. When I got my first driver's license in Czechoslovakia and later, my first car, I always took hitchhikers. I still do.

Let's talk about life in the camp at Neuhaus. There was a manager of this place. He was not a very friendly guy, but really he couldn't be. He had wall-to-wall people. Some might have been criminals. I believe some really were criminals. He advised us, "Guys, it would be a really good idea to go and get a job." We didn't have any work permits or papers to work legally in Austria. He said, "It doesn't matter. You should get a job on the black market. It is not good for you to sit all day and do nothing."

Getting a job was my intention in the first place anyway. I was not the type of guy to be sitting there playing cards and smoking all day and just waiting for a year or so to maybe be admitted to the United States. The reason why we were there was that we were being investigated by Austrian authorities – who we really were. They did not know if we were spies, or criminals or honest people. They already knew quite a bit because we gave up our passports when we were in isolation, where the process started. Most of us husbands were looking for a job and I mean any job. Some were hired in local restaurants as dishwashers or labor workers in construction. I got a job in a sawmill. It was very hard work and I will never forget it. My back is screwed up even today from this job. But I made more money in the two months I worked there than I was able to smuggle with me from Czechoslovakia.

The pay was a lot better in Austria in hard currency (Austrian shillings) compared to what I was making in Czech krons for a highly qualified job. Therefore we could buy extras for our kids. We were buying fresh fruit. We were going to the swimming pool in the neighboring town in the afternoon or on the weekends, and we could pay for admission. We also went on a trip to Vienna to see Vasek and his family a couple of times. Of course we were hitchhiking. We bought some new clothes and shoes, especially for the boys. One of the first things I bought in Austria was a 12-string guitar. I told Helena, "I need a guitar because a guitar is going to help us. Trust me. We cannot speak the language, but I can play music and I can sing. We will be treated differently." She finally agreed and said, "OK, go and buy your guitar." And since then I have always had a guitar. It has helped us make a lot of friends. It was a smart decision. I was happy.

I'm going back a little bit now. When I got to the camp for refugees, it was just about the time that I should have been back in Czechoslovakia. It was time for my vacation to have been over. My parents did not know that I was even on a "vacation" in Italy. But my friend Simon knew. He was not only instructed as to what to do with our goods that were stashed in his house, but he also had some letters from us to distribute. One was for my brother, giving him an explanation that we were gone, that we had escaped. I was telling him goodbye and not to give up on me. Helena had a letter for her mother and her sister. I asked my brother to explain everything to my parents, to also read his letter to them. Helena and I had spent a lot of time thinking about how we were going to write these letters because we knew that it was going to be very painful for our families to find out that we were gone. We had to compose these letters in such a way as to cause as little pain as possible. It is very difficult for people in the free world to imagine that we were leaving forever, never to be able to see our families again because of the political situation with the communists in power. We thought that this communist era wouldn't change in our lifetime. We thought the communists were there for generations to come. I told Simon that he could start to distribute these letters to these people two or three weeks after our "vacation" ended.

Next I had to write and send a letter to my parents to protect them from being suspects in our escape. I had composed a letter in my head, and I put it on paper while I was at the camp for refugees. It was a confession letter to my parents. It was a letter that they would have in their possession to show the authorities in Czechoslovakia so they would be cleared from the investigation and they would not be suspected of having helped me to escape. I stated in this letter, "My dear parents, I thank you very much for raising me up, and I always appreciated that you taught me how to love our country and the communist regime. I know that this will hurt you, but I have turned a different direction from what you taught me. I was on a vacation in Italy, and something happened with me while I was there. I just cannot turn back the other way now. I saw people from non-communist countries enjoying their lives, not having to count every penny when buying ice cream for their children, being happy and friendly to each other. Maybe I am so naïve, and maybe I am so gullible. But I am turning my back on all that you taught me. Please forgive me, but I decided not to come back to Czechoslovakia. I am going to go to America. Your loving son, George." My parents understood immediately from the first sentence that this was b...s.... They also knew from my brother, through Simon, the truth. But they had to play dumb. If they were investigated, they had this letter to keep the secret police from jumping all over them. It was a good thing that they had it, because that's exactly what happened – they were investigated.

The name "KGB" was kept as a big secret by the Russians – we knew there was a secret investigation agency run by them but we had never heard the term or the abbreviation. The police came and wanted to take my father to be interrogated at their station at Bartolomejska Street. This station had a very bad reputation. If anybody heard that someone was being taken there, it brought goose bumps because we knew this would be no picnic. When my brother heard that my father was being taken to Bartolomejska, he immediately got into the picture and "volunteered" to be present. He explained to the police that my father was in very poor health and very upset with what his son George had done. He told them that our father had already survived one heart attack and if they didn't want to call the funeral home, they needed him to be there to help answer their questions. My father presented my letter, the "proof" that my parents had no knowledge of anything. The police made a copy of the letter. My father and my brother were explaining how upset the whole family was that I had turned against them and against society. They told the police I was very bad, and that they were never expecting anything like this. In reality, we knew that our parents wished us well because we loved each other. Everyone really did a lot of crying, and Helena's mother took it the hardest. She probably never recovered because her first grandchild was George, Jr. She just couldn't get over it. She had lived so close to us. Later on, in her letters to us, she told us how her communist neighbors were making it very hard for her. They would say sarcastically and viciously, "Well, we hope that George and Helena already have a brand new house in America as nice as the one they left here." They never missed an opportunity to dig into her every time they could. I felt very sorry for her.

Let's go back and finish this story from the camp in Austria. After about two months, I was informed by mail and also by the manager of the camp, that I would have an important interview. What happened was one of the milestones that I will never forget. Two Austrian officials came to the camp. They knew everything about me. They knew my life story since I was born. They also knew where I was working on the black market. They knew my attitude. They brought a translator from German to Czech.

It became very emotional for me because when we were sitting there, they said, "Mr. Stastny, you have been cleared by the Austrian government, and we would like to welcome you to start your new life in Austria." Just remembering this makes a huge lump in my throat. It was so, so nice to hear that we were welcome. You need to understand that Europe is different from America. America is made up of people who have come from all over the world. European countries are different – once a refugee, always a refugee. And here were these Austrian officials opening their arms and welcoming us to become a part of their country. They were really working hard to keep us in Austria. But I was very determined to go to the United States. I said, "I am so thankful. I appreciate so much all of your help. But I made a decision a long time ago that I would go to the United States." They tried again, again, and again. They told me how much help I was going to get from the Austrians – how much easier it was going to be. They told me that the children could go to Czech schools in Austria and would get so much assistance. They also started talking about the numbers of holidays in Austria compared to the few holidays in the United States. They were not putting the United States down, not at all. They were just comparing a lot of facts. But I was stubborn. Then they said, "Well, in that case, regrettably, we must inform you that we have to turn your papers over to representatives of the United States, and the whole process has to start all over again. So far you have only been investigated by the Austrians. In the meantime, you will have to stay in the camp." I thought, "Oh, well." I was not happy to hear this, but I knew I couldn't do anything about it. I really showed my appreciation to them, and I thanked them again for what their country was doing for us.

Many people have asked me why I was so sure I wanted to come to the United States. Well, I had a connection in McMinnville, Oregon – my friend Louie, who had escaped in 1966, as well as two Americans, Cleo and Ed Tomco. You already know quite a bit about Louie, but now I must explain about Cleo and Ed. Louie escaped in 1966 and after a couple of years, he was drafted into the U.S. Army and stationed in Alaska. A ski competition was being held and several non-English speaking Czechs were competing. A translator was needed for them and somehow Louie was enlisted to do this. At the same time, Ed Tomco, who was originally from Slovakia (Czech and Slovak are very similar languages) and who was very well known in the Anchorage area, volunteered to help also. Louie and Ed met and soon became very good friends even though Ed was a generation older. After this ski event, Louie was invited to Ed and Cleo's home for dinner and this was the beginning of their long relationship.

Ed was a teacher and administrator. They had six children, and Louie fit right in. They did not legally adopt Louie, but he became like a family member. Ed had been brought to this country at the age of six by his uncle. Ed had this connection to Slovakia and Cleo loved to travel. She now had a really good reason to travel to Czechoslovakia because of Louie and Ed's backgrounds. She came to Czechoslovakia by herself a number of times, and one time she looked me up and brought me a message of greeting from Louie. She told me Louie was their family friend. This was way before I had made any plans for escaping. It was about the time I was finishing building the house, that I met her for the first time.

The second time I met her, our house was finished and I invited her to come for an evening of music and fun. We couldn't speak English and she didn't speak Czech, but we had a good time. I was playing guitar and banjo, and we were singing American songs with Czech words. She sang the same songs in English. We showed a lot of pictures to each other, which was a great way to communicate. She was showing me pictures of Louie, which I was very happy to see after so many years. She was very approachable to any kind of conversation.

Cleo was very interested in the history of WWII, especially with the underground resistance of the Czech paratroopers trained in England to assassinate SS General Reinhard Heydrich. This incredibly cruel 37-year-old beast had been personally appointed by Hitler to rule Czechoslovakia. I took Cleo to show her where the assassination took place. It was very interesting to me, even though we were using only hand language, how much she knew about this story. I always thought of Cleo as a friend, even though I only saw her twice.

When we were in the camp for refugees, I felt that was the time to inform Cleo and Louie that we had escaped and wanted to come to the U.S.A. I was thinking about writing a letter to Cleo, but I had a hard time with English, so with the help of one person in the camp who knew English quite well, I sent a short telegram to her. I wrote, "Hello, Cleo. I am in Austria. We escaped from Czechoslovakia. We want to come to U.S., George."

It was very short, but I thought it was clear. The answer from Cleo came also as a telegram. It came back immediately and it said, "George, you are welcome with the whole family, Cleo." This is very hard for me to talk about – please give me a few moments…

There I was in the camp for refugees being encouraged to stay in Austria. We had also become friends with Vasek's family in Vienna. They even came to see us in the camp and also wanted us to stay in Austria. Our kids had become friends with their daughter. Vasek was pointing out all the pluses and advantages that Austria had compared to other countries. At one point, he said, "George, I heard that in the U.S. you won't get any help from the government. It is like throwing a cat into the water and telling it to swim." He meant it well and wanted to protect us – he didn't want anything bad to happen to us. I felt so lucky to be surrounded with such good people. With people who cared and wanted to help and they did help.

When I made my original plan to go to the U.S., I knew that I would like to be somewhere close to Louie and Cleo (they lived in the same area in Oregon). But I didn't want to impose on them or bother them. I thought it would have been very helpful to settle somewhere in Portland or Salem, but Cleo's reaction was overwhelming. She wanted to help so much and immediately. Louie and Ed were in Alaska at that time working for the Alaskan pipeline. It was Louie's main job and Ed's, as a retired educator, summer job to make extra money. Cleo contacted them both and I believe, with her big input, they decided that Cleo and Ed Tomco were going to sponsor us because they had a larger house and were financially stronger than Louie. It was a very big and very generous offer.

At that time I didn't have much knowledge about what it really meant to be a sponsor. But six years later, I became very much aware of that because I became a sponsor myself for another person. Sponsorship comes with a big responsibility – before the newcomers get established, providing housing and food if necessary, helping to find employment, introducing newcomers to and helping them learn about American society, supervising their learning of the English language. Being a sponsor of legal immigrants requires a signed guarantee that these newcomers will not become homeless and a burden on the U.S. government.

When I made that first decision to escape from Czechoslovakia and go to the U.S.A., my mind was very much occupied with the escape plans and all the arrangements. But at the same time, I started to collect as much information about the U.S. as I could. There was not much available under communism. I studied U.S. geography from the world atlas and I started to learn a little – a very little bit – of English from an English dictionary. Most of it was just vocabulary.

I would like to explain another reason why I was so sure I wanted to come to the United States. I never had any interest to live in any German-speaking country. Since I was a child, I had too much negative feeling in my system about Germans. I was too much influenced by the WWII atrocities that the Germans committed on innocent people, including Czechs. My grandparents lived only one mile from the concentration camp Terezin, which made a huge negative impact on our whole family. On the other hand, I heard enough positive things about America from my family and friends, plus the fact that Louie and Cleo's family were there. That was a very natural decision to me to want to live in the U.S. But even if I wouldn't have been welcomed by Cleo, Ed and Louie, I would still have wanted to go to the U.S. and start my new life there. However, I am sure I would have ended up somewhere else, wherever a sponsor would be found. I was always very stubborn about coming to the U.S. And I don't think there is anything wrong with being stubborn!

19

An Interview in the U.S. Embassy

I was working very hard in the small local sawmill, working long hours and many times on the weekends, too. I was coming home to the camp exhausted, achy, especially my back, but happy to be earning money for my family. This small mill had only one, but very good quality, cutter, and it was amazing to me how effective and productive it was. There were only five of us running it. If this had been in Czechoslovakia, there would be probably at least 15-20 people running the cutter and still not producing any more because of the work ethic.

The owner was working with us, operating a big loader. It looked like a huge forklift with special forks. He was bringing logs from piles and placing them on the chute that moved the logs by gravity right into the cutter. The cutter operator was a skilled worker who knew about anything and everything. When the lumber was cut and spilled out of the cutter, there was me with another guy, and our job was to lift these very heavy pieces and throw them on the conveyor belt that moved them to the last person who cut them on the sides and stacked them into bundles. Then the owner removed the bundles with the forklift. We all were important to run the sawmill, but the most important was the owner who regulated the speed at which we worked, and he was working fast. There was no way any of us could take a break or slow down. This was the very first time where I saw the difference in the work ethic under communism where no one cared and the work ethic under a private owner. It showed on productivity and our pay. We worked hard and even though I was the lowest paid employee, I made very good money. For me it was, "George, welcome to the world of free enterprise!" I liked it! At the end of my shift, I walked a mile back to the camp, and I felt good about how much we had accomplished during the day.

Then one day, the manager of the camp came to me and explained that we had gotten an invitation to the U.S. Embassy. It was such good news. I was so happy and excited, and I have to admit, I was full of hope. The manager also emphasized that we needed to look very presentable. He said, "You are a good man because you follow the rules. I wish you luck." This was the guy that everybody called Gestapo. Nobody liked him. I didn't like him either, but I realized that his job was not very easy. I understood that he had to be strict, and I never complained.

For instance, this happened a number of times. As I mentioned before we had one small room for the four of us. It was old and ugly when we moved in. We decorated the room as much as possible with whatever was available. We always kept it clean. Our room was simply but very nicely furnished with next to nothing. So, the manager, when he needed to show his bosses how he was providing for people, always took them and showed them our room. We always made up our beds with our sleeping bags. I absolutely hate a mess. So did Helena. I guess Czech people are cleaning freaks! We even took our shoes off when we came into the room, even though the floor was damaged. That is a Czech custom anyway, to take your shoes off in your house.

We were waiting for this invitation for some time and I knew that this would be a huge and very important milestone for us. We couldn't take the chance of messing up, so we took this invitation very seriously. We prepared ourselves, dressed up the best we could, told the boys that they must behave and be absolutely quiet, and then we reported to the U.S. Embassy. I remember when we were in the waiting room, my heart was pounding. I tried to be calm but questions were spinning in my head. What was this extremely important interview going to look like? What kinds of questions would they ask me? How long would this take? Will I do well? I was trying to keep my cool but I didn't know if I could. Finally a door opened and we were invited into the room where some sort of official was sitting. He was an American and I knew immediately, just by looking at him, that he was a decision maker. There was also another person, the official translator. Even people who spoke good English had to have a translator because these interviews were so important. There could be something in the language where you might say "maybe," or "I could," or "I would," and your life course could turn a different direction. The translator told us that he would translate everything very carefully and advised me to take time before I answered, to be very patient and specific. I had been studying English very hard while I was in the camp for refugees, but all I really understood and could say in English at that moment was "hello" plus a few numbers and everyday phrases.

This meeting started. The decision maker already knew about my background and had all my paperwork in front of him. He had probably studied it before he came in. Then he started with his questions. "What can you do for the United States? What will the United States gain by admitting you? How will you act if you lose your job? What would you do? What are you going to do if your family struggles? How are you going to provide? What are your plans? What is your attitude about getting help from the U.S. government? Are you healthy? Have you ever had any disease? Have you been involved with any weapons?" There were all kinds of questions. He probably already knew things like I was not a criminal and that I was never a communist, that nobody from our family had been a member of the Communist Party. He asked a lot of other questions. I think that even though I was quite nervous and sweaty (who wouldn't be at this very important moment), I answered his questions confidently. Basically I answered that I was very proud of my parents, that they taught me what's right and what's wrong. They taught me to work very hard. I told him that I was 36 years old, and I'd learned in my life a number of various skills that I would use to provide for my family. I added that I enjoyed working, and I would work very hard and probably for the rest of my life. I told him my goal was to successfully raise my family. I assured him that if I were allowed to live in the U.S., I would be a very proud and productive citizen. I also assured him that I was not expecting any financial or any other form of support from the U.S. or any other government. When I finished with my answers, this official didn't say anything. He didn't say yes or no. After a moment of silence, he said, "OK. Thank you very much." He turned to Helena – he had not asked her any questions so far. And he asked her only this, "Do you agree with everything your husband said?" She said, "Yes." Then he shuffled the paperwork in front of him for a while and told us, "You are going to go right from here to the hospital. Your whole family will go through all these exams and get x-rays. We will contact you after we get the results. Thank you very much. Goodbye."

He gave us a map of Vienna and a whole bunch of papers requesting all kinds of health exams in the hospital. When he left the room, the translator whispered to me, "I think you are on a very good track. So far everything is going right. Now it depends on the results of your medical tests. If all the tests come back negative, there is a very good chance you will be allowed to go to America." I felt very encouraged and very relieved. I felt like I had just won the final qualifying race to be able to go to the Olympic Games!

After all these medical exams were finished, we went back to the refugee camp. We now had a period of waiting time and the excitement and expectations were high. In a couple of weeks, we got the results back, and we got a very official looking registered mail from the U.S. Embassy. It was so exciting that my hands were shaking. Helena and I were looking at each other and said, "This is it! Let's open it!" I crossed myself, opened the letter and there was the very good news. The U.S. Embassy notified us that we had been admitted to the United States of America. I am getting choked up just thinking about this!

We were given a departure date – October 6, 1980. Our plane would be leaving at such and such time, and we would be on it. They made all the arrangements. We would owe some money for the trip. It was not actually that much because some Catholic charity chipped in and helped to pay for part of it. When I finished reading this letter, I had to sit down and catch a deep breath. We were so happy. It was such good news. And then we were just jumping for joy. We had worked on this for so long and had dreamt about it and now the time had finally arrived. It was a huge landmark in our lives. **WE WILL GO TO AMERICA!!** We were very pleased and immediately contacted Cleo and told her that we can come and we are coming!

At this point, we knew it was time to tell the boys what exactly was going on. This was not an easy thing to do. They were too young to understand the political situation in communist Czechoslovakia, which meant a very uncertain future for them. They were living in their protected child-like world, surrounded by family love, their friends and their toys. Helena and I were trying in the most clever and gentle way to tell them that we would never be going back to Czechoslovakia. Even though we tried to emphasize a positive and exciting future, like flying on a jet plane (they had never flown), seeing a big ocean and mountains, luring them on the most positive things – even though we were saying all this to them, they still reacted with shock. The younger one, Martin (seven) started to cry immediately. We tried to pacify him as much as we could. The older one, George, Jr. (nine), tried to take the news without crying, like a hero. We promised both boys that we would establish ourselves in the U.S. with everything that they had had in Czechoslovakia, including a new home with their toys and a new family of friends. It took some time, and both boys slowly got used to this new course of events.

1980 was a hard year for the boys because we had been traveling from place to place and each time, they had made friends and then had to leave them – at the beach, in Vienna, at the camp for refugees. We were at the camp the longest (four months) and they were adjusting to Austrian society, even picking up a little bit of German. We knew that we would have to be gentle and still work with them on what was going to happen, and we did.

20

The Dream Finally Comes True!

October 6 was another "D-Day" for our long journey and it was coming fast. We were preparing ourselves for the completely unknown, but we hoped for the best. I studied English as much as I could and for that reason, I stopped working in the sawmill. I gave them plenty of notice, but the sawmill owner was not happy to hear that. He personally came to the camp trying to make me stay and work longer. He even offered me more money. It was a very difficult situation for both of us. I really needed time to prepare ourselves for our big departure.

We still had our car in front of the camp that I wanted to sell. Our car was not really big and fancy but it was relatively new and in good shape. I'm sure that here in the U.S. you would probably laugh to see that car sitting somewhere next to some big Cadillac or pickup truck. But back in Czechoslovakia, it was a very nice, popular, and expensive car – two-cycle engine, 900 cc, three-cylinder made in East Germany. It was not a Trabant; it was a Wartburg. The sale was very difficult because the car didn't have Austrian documents. I sold it for very little – I didn't have a choice – to the daughter of one of the local photographers with whom we had become friends. He was a Czech immigrant, probably 15 years older than me, from a long, long time ago. By the way, he told me when we were leaving, "George, Czechoslovakia is a small country, but you will find Czechs everywhere you go." This photographer and I kept exchanging Christmas cards, and we kept in contact for quite some time. Fifteen years later, he wrote to me that the car gave up and they had to trash it. We don't keep in contact anymore, which is too bad. I don't know if he is alive or if he is well. Someday I would like to go back and find him. I know that his name is Vaclav Fejt. People would know him because he took pictures of everybody's weddings and high school graduations.

October 6 was approaching fast. We were preparing ourselves for our departure. Just to give you a little idea what we needed to do – we were still dressed and equipped for summer camping in Italy. We all needed better and warmer clothes. We needed two suitcases for more clothes, shoes, miscellaneous belongings, and a few gifts for Cleo, Ed and Louie. I was also taking my new guitar and of course, the banjo my brother had made for me. We had to move our traveling luggage to the main camp in Traiskirchen two days in advance of our departure. The rest of our stuff, like our primitive camping furniture and the boys' toys, we gave to people in the Neuhaus camp. Then we made an arrangement with one young single man who had a tiny little car to take us very early on October 6 back to Traiskirchen. This car was so little we barely fit. We were literally like a can of sardines. The car was also kind of a clunker and since this was a very important time for me, I worried if we would make it.

It was not easy to say good-bye to our new camp friends, but the most difficult was saying good-bye to Vasek in Vienna and his family. I don't like saying good-bye to friends, but this good-bye to Vasek was especially hard. We were sure that we would not see each other again. We gave each other long hugs with a lot of tears. We were also being torn apart emotionally for other reasons. I would say for a geographical reason. So far, we were in Austria, a neighboring country to Czechoslovakia. But now we were leaving the European continent, crossing the Atlantic Ocean, going to America and then again, crossing the whole continent, all the way to the opposite side of the world, to Oregon.

Our itinerary took us from Vienna to London, London to New York, New York to Salt Lake City, and from Salt Lake City to Portland, Oregon. I had difficulty communicating because I didn't speak enough English. I spoke a little bit of German having been in Austria for four months. It was not that difficult in Austria, but when we landed in London all I could say were things like, "Where bathroom?" I needed to ask, "Where is our terminal? What is the number of our flight?" But I couldn't because I was so limited. It was confusing and very difficult.

When we were getting on our plane in Vienna, there was a little episode. We were being bussed to the plane that was sitting on the tarmac, but our whole family didn't fit into one bus because of the large crowd of people. I was in one bus with both children, but Helena couldn't get on that bus. She had to wait for the next one. Helena and I understood that, but the children started to cry hysterically. They knew we were leaving for the United States, but they thought she didn't get on the bus and we will be leaving her behind. I had to pacify them. When you are seven and nine years old and you have never flown before, you don't know what to expect. They cried until she showed up on the plane. This plane belonged to Austrian Airlines. There were several other refugees from the main camp on this plane flying to London. Some would then continue on to Canada, but most of the passengers were normal civilians. The flight attendants were aware that we were political refugees, and they came to us and advised us that if we had to have an emergency landing in any communist country, we should absolutely not leave the plane under any circumstances, only in case of fire. We would be arrested on the spot. It was a very difficult and mixed feeling, especially when we flew over Czechoslovakia. Looking down on the land where we were born was very hard. Knowing that our loved ones were still there was incredibly difficult. My thoughts were revolving in my head that we would never see our loved ones again. It was a very emotional time for us. But on the other hand, I had a very good feeling that I will never have to see communists and the Iron Curtain again.

We landed in London and got on the next plane (TWA) to New York. This type of traveling was totally new to us. I was on a plane a couple of times before and Helena had flown once, but always on small prop planes in Czechoslovakia. To get around the airport in London was a challenge for us, but luckily, we managed. The plane from London to New York was a 747 jumbo jet. I couldn't get over the size of this plane and the number of passengers. We were well-fed and could watch a movie while flying – I was totally amazed at all these comforts. We could purchase headphones for $4 but that was a lot of money for us. Since we couldn't speak English, we wouldn't have understood anything anyway, so we just enjoyed watching the pictures. Most of the time, I was watching how everything worked on the plane. We didn't have window seats but I remember that there was a group of soldiers whose captain had a window seat. He was looking at us, and it must have been obvious to him that we were flying for the first time. He generously offered us his seat and we took turns sitting by the window.

The flight to New York was a long flight but it went by very fast because I had plenty of things to explore. I was very concerned about getting on the next plane in New York, but as it turned out, the Catholic charity took really good care of us. They arranged the transfer from one plane to another plane. They sent an old Czech gentleman, who had immigrated years and years ago. He was waiting for us at the gate in New York. He had a sign with our name on it and took us by the hand to our next gate. I appreciated his service because it was so far away; we had to take a short ride in a taxi. We were processed by U.S. officers as we were getting to our gate. There was a little embarrassing situation for us. We didn't have any problem with our documents, but an officer asked us if we had any food with us. We didn't understand the question so this lady started to open our carry-on luggage. She found some sandwiches made of meat loaf that she unwrapped. We had carried these from early morning and the sandwiches were really messy. She looked at us, looked at the sandwiches, back and forth two or three times. We knew that she didn't want us to travel with this food, but looking at our little and hungry boys, she decided we could have them, quickly rewrapped them and said "Go!"

We got on the next plane to Portland, Oregon, with a stop in Salt Lake City. We didn't have to changes planes in Salt Lake, but had a wait of about 45 minutes there. It was already dark, Martin was sleeping, but George, Jr. and I were snooping around the plane. Everything to us was new and exciting. One of the pilots noticed us and started to ask some questions, but we didn't understand a word. He figured out that this was exciting for us to be on this plane. Unexpectedly, he opened the cockpit and invited us in. What an awesome moment! He let us sit in the pilot and co-pilot seats. Even though we didn't speak the language, we understood not to touch anything except the steering wheel. I was amazed at how many gauges were in the cockpit. George, Jr. and I were looking at each other and pretending that we were flying. The entire flight crew and all Americans we had met so far impressed me with their friendliness. We returned to our assigned seats, the plane took off and we were on the last leg of our flight to Portland, Oregon. I knew about Oregon only from a map. When we were landing in Portland, it was dark and I saw all the lights and thought, "This is our new home." I knew McMinnville was somewhere close but I didn't know how far and I didn't know what to expect. We all were excited about meeting Cleo, and the boys knew she was going to be their new "aunt."

21

Early Days in McMinnville, Oregon

When we landed in Portland, we got out of the plane. Here were four refugees – two parents with two small kids, two suitcases, a guitar and a banjo. We had prepared the kids that Cleo would be waiting for us, and we were all excited to see her. She was waiting for us at the gate and she had with her, their youngest child, 17-year-old daughter Gretchen. I had met Gretchen once in Prague when she was 11. She had grown up and looked very different – she was a pretty young lady. From 11 to 17 is a big difference! It was very exciting when we all saw each other. There was a lot of hugging and "talking" but in two different languages. Happiness was in the air. I started to count people and our luggage and started to worry that we wouldn't fit into Cleo's car. I knew that our car that we had in Czechoslovakia would not handle everyone and everything. We thought our Czech car was pretty big at that time. I had seen some American cars in Austria, but they were still quite small compared to when I saw Cleo's car. I just couldn't believe my eyes! She led us to her car which was a full-sized Ford LTD. It was one of the biggest cars in the row of cars parked there. She walked around and opened the door and the trunk. The trunk was as big as my whole car in Czechoslovakia! After all my worries, we didn't have any problem for all of us to fit in, and Cleo started to drive to McMinnville, which took a little more than an hour and a half to get to their home.

On the way to our new home, we all were trying very hard to communicate, but it wasn't easy. 1½ hours was a long time. Even though I had started to study a little bit of English in Czechoslovakia when I made the decision to escape and live in the U.S., it was not enough. At that time I was very busy preparing for our escape. I had started to study English more intensively in the camp for refugees. And again, I was busy working, being too tired, and because of many different events, I couldn't concentrate on this study. Most of my study was just learning new vocabulary. The problem was that I didn't know how to pronounce the words correctly, and I must have had a very strong accent. I also didn't know anything about making a sentence. My new language experience in the last two days of traveling had been very frustrating. I was realizing more and more that knowledge of English was now a question of life or death, success or failure.

It was close to midnight and more than 40 hours without any sleep for us. We were very tired! When we got to McMinnville and Tomco's house, it was obvious to me from the very beginning that Cleo must have put so much work into our arrival. So much planning and preparation. They gave us the rec room of their house for us to stay in. It was very generous of them. We were exhausted, so after a very short tour of their house, we went to sleep right away. I need to mention that when we got to their house, Ed was not there. As I mentioned before, he was in Alaska working during the summer on the pipeline to make some extra money. Since this was now October, he was close to being finished and to returning to McMinnville. My long-time friend, Louie, was living in Oregon, in Amity just outside of McMinnville. But he was also in Alaska working on the pipeline. He was coming home a little bit later than Ed. We were with Cleo for about two weeks in her house before Ed came home from Alaska.

My good friends and sponsors, Cleo and Ed Tomco.

The first day we didn't do much. Cleo took us to downtown McMinnville (population about 12,000 in 1980; 33,000 in 2010) and we walked around a bit. We ate a sandwich in the local deli and went into a few stores. We walked around her neighborhood. McMinnville was definitely a different town than Prague. We were kind of shocked. There were no buses, no streetcars, no subways, and almost no traffic. Another first impression was that there weren't any crowds on the sidewalks – Americans weren't walking – they were driving everywhere! McMinnville was a small, pretty and clean town with very much of a Western flavor in our opinion. I was looking and looking to see if I can see some cowboys on horses riding through the streets! I didn't see any but I saw something almost as exciting – many pickup trucks being driven by people who looked like cowboys. I had never seen pickups before – there weren't any in Europe at this time, and they were completely new to me. McMinnville made a good first impression on us.

George, Jr. and Martin – first week in McMinnville – in new shirts.

We were fighting jet lag, so this first day was a recovery day. The following day, we already knew that the kids were going to go to school. Cleo took us to Columbus School near her house to enroll the boys. We all were dressed well. We met our boys' new teachers, the principal and the school secretary.

Cleo did all the talking and we did a lot of smiling. Carolyn was one of those two new teachers, and I will give her the opportunity to explain to you about her experiences and memories.

But first, I need to clarify that Carolyn and I had a very good parent-teacher relationship for a number of years despite my language barrier. I wanted to help with anything that the boys' teachers needed like chaperoning at the swimming pool or with the Christmas program. For my good feeling, I need to emphasize that we started to date after my divorce from Helena.

(Now this is Carolyn speaking...) My teaching partner, Brad Mills, and I had heard from the principal that we would be getting a new non-English speaking student. We already had five kids from southeast Asia who were ESL (English as a Second Language) students, so I thought one more wouldn't matter all that much. Then I heard this child was Czech and thought, "Humm, I speak fair German – it shouldn't be any problem to communicate with this young man since it is a neighboring country." How wrong I was. Czech isn't even remotely related to German! George, Jr. came into my classroom, a shy nine-year-old. This was in mid-October, 1980. By the end of June and the school year, he was speaking very passable English and making great progress in his studies. He was a really good kid and a very ambitious and conscientious student. He took his studies very seriously. He quickly made friends with his new classmates and was fitting very nicely into the culture of our fourth grade classroom. Two years later, I had transferred to sixth grade, so I had the privilege of having George, Jr. in my class again. By then, it was hard to realize he had only been speaking English for two years – he sounded and acted just like all the rest of the sixth graders! During George, Jr.'s first year, I was also the school music teacher and had decided to do an adaptation of "The Nutcracker" for our school's Christmas program. Since every child in the school was to be involved, and George, Jr.'s English was just beginning, I made him a clown for one of the dances and he was thrilled. Martin was placed in a second grade classroom but I was also his music teacher. I remember that Martin was NOT a shy kid, but rather had a bit of the devil in him, but always with a huge grin on his face.

(Back to George, Sr.) Our boys really liked their new American school. They also liked school buses, which didn't exist in Europe. When George, Jr. came home from his second day of school, he was telling us excitedly that Mr. Mills had ordered all the desks be put on the side so everyone could play soccer in the classroom. The "ball" was made out of crunched paper so no one would get hurt, and the teacher played with them! Both boys were so pleased with the freedom and friendliness of their American classrooms, unlike the very strict and regimented Czech classrooms.

I had no idea what my job would be, but I was ready to go to work. That was a big part of the reason why I was here. The problem was that there was no job for me. But I didn't know this. Cleo did not have a job for me. I had no idea what she would have to go through when she said she would be my sponsor. In Austria they asked if I had a sponsor or if I wanted them to find one for me. I told them about Cleo, but I had no idea about what I was getting her into. I thought a sponsor was some kind of a person you would hang out with, no commitments or strings attached. The U.S. Immigration office contacted her and asked if she would agree to be our sponsor. When Cleo received the paperwork from them, she found out that one of the requirements, besides many others, was that there needed to be a job available for me. But she was a retired lady, and she and Ed had recently moved to Oregon from Alaska and didn't know anyone yet except their immediate neighbors. There was no way for her to find a job for me.

One of Cleo's neighbors, Doug Rose, was a pastor of a nearby church and heard about her dilemma. He spoke to his congregation one Sunday and explained about Cleo's situation. He said that his neighbor was going to sponsor a family who had escaped from communist Czechoslovakia. The pastor further explained that we were sitting in a camp for refugees and that they wanted to get us here as soon as possible. He told them that one of the requirements was to have a job for me and asked the congregation if anyone could provide this. He told them the skills I had and also had to tell them that I spoke no English. The whole congregation got excited, but no one could provide a job for me. However, there was a logger named Don Endicott, who came to the pastor and to Cleo and explained that he would have a job for me at this time, but he wasn't 100% sure if the job situation would not change before I would arrive in the U.S. Nevertheless, he assured the pastor and Cleo that he could sign the paper, which was important for the time being. Our stay would have been much longer in the camp otherwise. But at that time, I did not know about all of this because of language. Cleo and I were communicating on a very simple level and I found out the details later on.

22

Refugee Camp Rumors and Cleo's Help

To be really honest with you, I don't think that we were in the camp for refugees for a long time. You can look at the four months two different ways. It's a long time to be a refugee in a camp, but it's a relatively short time for a refugee to be processed and to get permission to go to the U.S. I would like to tell you that every day, when we were in the camp, we heard a new rumor about which countries were open to refugees and which were not. We would hear that Canada was going to stop taking refugees. We would hear that America did not provide any support and was the hardest country to start over in. We heard that Canada had a lot of social programs to help refugees but America would not give you anything. We also heard that Australia was one of the countries that was easy to get into and you would get a lot of help. I didn't understand the way of thinking of some of the refugees. They were just focusing on the benefits they would get.

There was no way that I could be persuaded to think about Australia, West Germany, Switzerland, or Canada. I always had some kind of answer for these rumors. I always wanted to go to the U.S. – I never changed my mind. I knew it was not going to be easy, and I always said, "I am going to go to work. I am not looking for some handout. I am not looking for some kind of charity. I want to work and start a new life." I always liked the U.S., and I believed very strongly that I would fit into this society and I would be a productive citizen. I thought and believed it was going to work. Some refugees were changing their minds about what country they wanted to be living in. Some people even changed their minds more than once. To me, they looked like some "country-hoppers" and as a result, in my opinion, no country wanted them because the representatives of these countries saw so many changes on their processing documents. The officials were not interested in people like that, so the documents were put on the back burner. Consequently, these people were waiting and waiting in the camp for a very long time, in some cases, more than two years. Some people just couldn't stop yakking about that all the time, like they didn't have anything else to do. As a result, they created a really difficult and scary atmosphere.

But there were also very serious situations, and they were not rumors at all. This is a good time to mention one. There was one father who escaped from Czechoslovakia with his two young daughters approximately seven and twelve years of age, leaving his wife behind. We were all getting used to living in a free country on the other side of the Iron Curtain. We were protective of our children, but not paranoid that someone would come and steal them. This father's plan was to go to Canada but he didn't know how long it would take to do the processing, so he put the girls in the local Austrian school. Each day these girls were walking from the camp to school and back again until one day the older girl came running frantically and screaming back to camp that someone had kidnapped her sister. The police were called immediately and the camp was swarming with police cars.

The news traveled really fast and everyone was hanging onto their children. The police were questioning the older girl, wanting to know exactly what had happened. She described a car with some strangers in it behind the school and said she saw her sister willingly get into that car and then the car took off. This had happened in the early afternoon when school was out. For the rest of the day until late in the evening, the police and this father didn't have any answers until this father called his ex-wife in Czechoslovakia to tell her that their younger daughter had been kidnapped. Her response was, "Yes, I know. That was my plan. The kidnappers were the Czech secret police, and they asked our daughter if she wanted to see me. Of course, I wasn't in the car, but they had her and promised her they would drive her to see me." This woman was a communist and the father was not. She got the younger daughter because she knew they would never be able to get the older one who would kick, scream and resist. Because the distance from the Czech border to the camp was manageable, it wasn't at all difficult for these Czech communist agents to do this. As a result of this experience, even though we were in a free country, we all had doubts about our safety. This was one more instance that showed how stressful it was for all of us, having escaped communism, then being refugees and not knowing what the future held and then something like this happens. Sometimes I felt like a fugitive.

Let's get back to Oregon, in McMinnville, when I wanted to start to work. I was very anxious to get a job, and I felt responsible to provide for my family. I hate to admit this, but I know that I had a very hard time to be patient. I felt like I was so much behind. I was 36 years old, the time when most people had already established their careers and here I was, not speaking the language, not having a job. I should have been building a nest for my family and I was hearing, "Take it easy! Don't worry. Everything is going to be fine." Well, I tried to be cool and look relaxed, but this time, I don't think I was a very good actor. I felt like time was being wasted. I was also calculating that soon we would run out of money. So, not having a job was very, very hard for me. Everyday, Cleo was telling me to take it easy – to wait for Louie to come back from Alaska. Since the job with the logger didn't work out, she wanted me to wait, saying that Louie would be back in about three weeks. Remember, this was the time before cell phones. She couldn't call Louie since he was working on the pipeline in Alaska in the middle of nowhere. It had to be Louie calling her when he had a chance. One time when Cleo was talking to Louie on the phone, she asked Louie to explain to me that she didn't have a job for me. Well, it was very exciting talking to Louie. I hadn't talked to him for 14 years! We both were glad to hear each other, but then he needed to explain to me that I didn't have a job. He didn't get into any details and it wouldn't have mattered to me anyway. I wouldn't blame anybody. I didn't know anything about a sponsor's responsibilities at that time, but for some reason, I thought that my job was lined up. Or if not, I could go anywhere and just get some job by myself. Louie convinced me to wait for him until he got back to Oregon, so after all, I did.

Cleo cooked for us and we tried to help as much as we could. We also tried to help financially. We had brought some money with us that I had made in Austria in the sawmill. I remember when we helped Cleo to do some grocery shopping. She always wanted to pay for everything but we insisted that we wanted to help, so she let us. I also wanted to pay her immediately for our flights. It was $1,200. I put it in front of her on the kitchen counter, and I told her it was for the airline tickets. She hadn't paid for them, but I didn't know that. I didn't understand all this process. I had been told in Austria that I would have to pay for the flights, and I thought I owed Cleo. Cleo, however, said emphatically, "No, no, no. I had nothing to do with that. Just keep your money." I found out later that Catholic charities had paid for our tickets, so we kept our money because we needed it and eventually, by paying a little at a time, we paid our obligation. Helena should get the credit for doing this – she was very responsible.

Cleo helped me open a checking account with the $1,200. I would like to mention that until then, I had never had a checking account. It was common in Czechoslovakia to have a savings account but not a checking account. People there always dealt with cash. Personal checks didn't exist. We were even being paid at work with cash. When I was working in the electronics factory as a supply officer, one of my responsibilities was to go twice a month on payday to receive all the money in cash for all the workers in our department, approximately 60+ people. I had to recount all this cash that I received to make sure there was no mistake, and then to sack it into the workers' envelopes by their pay stubs. People never had any checks in their pay envelopes – they didn't exist.

But now back to Cleo. She was doing a lot of things to help us. At the time she got the first telegram letting her know about our plan to come to the U.S., Cleo was being visited by an old friend from out-of-state. This lady looked at Cleo and said, "I guess you'd better start to cook and freeze food. You will have a family of four to feed. I will help you. Let's get started." This was one example showing Cleo's excitement in helping us. She was so wonderful.

Another example, and a very important one, was all the work Cleo did to help me learn English. I needed to learn English as fast as possible and I thought about that a lot. I hope that you are not tired of me talking about English so often. Please don't be, because this is a huge obstacle that follows you for years. Learning a new language is a very slow process, especially for adults. It takes an average of three years to be able to communicate on a simple level. It takes at least six years to be fluent. Of course, it depends on each person's talent and assuming that the person is willing to learn. So to help myself, I came up with an idea that I thought would speed up the process. I thought that I had invented something new, but later I found out that someone else had the same idea and used this before me. I made hundreds of small cards – on one side I wrote a word in Czech and on the other side, I wrote the same word in English. Cleo spent a lot of time with me, randomly pulling cards out of the box, holding them in front of me one by one with the English toward her and the Czech toward me. I had to say the word in English. She had control if I was saying the right word and pronouncing it correctly. That was my way to learn more vocabulary. Cleo was very patient. She spent a lot of time with me and Helena trying to communicate. With our limited ability, it was not easy at first, and it was frustrating for all of us. But Cleo was very persistent and it was good for us.

The knowledge of English is extremely important for immigrants.

Besides, we needed to be able to communicate with Cleo since we were living in her house. We were doing many things together, like cooking, washing clothes, talking about the boys' school, grocery shopping, going to the post office, etc. As time passed, it was getting easier and easier because many activities were repeating and so were our short and simple sentences. But sometimes, it was very difficult and frustrating when we needed to discuss some important and complicated subjects. For instance, if our children were vaccinated in Czechoslovakia and what kind of vaccinations for what kind of diseases. Or trying to understand the driver's manual, preparing myself for an American driving test. Or getting insurance. At those times, not even a dictionary was much help. But we got through it. Later, when I was able to put little sentences together, Cleo just loved to sit down in the late evening when all the chores were finished and talk to me, just to visit. We got into this habit, and even a year or so later, when we had our own house, I came from time to time to their house in the evening and visited with her. I always felt welcome! And we both enjoyed each other's company.

The knowledge of English is very important. Let me take a little sidetrack because I have something on my mind. Should I say this or not? I mean well, so I hope that you will understand. We are all living in this beautiful country voluntarily, and we should be speaking one language, English. That is part of the package that we knew about before we came here. I want to mention one example that was happening in our local building supply store, Lowe's, just recently.

All the announcements were being broadcast on the store intercom in two languages, English and Spanish. I didn't agree with that so I asked to speak to the manager. She explained to me that they want to HELP the Hispanic population. I told her first, that I like people from Mexico and some of them are very good friends of mine. But these Spanish announcements are not helping anybody, and especially in the long run. Many Spanish-speaking people would never learn English. They would think, "Why should I bother?" But they are hurting themselves, limiting themselves and therefore, they will always struggle.

Now back to our first days in McMinnville. Despite the fact that I had no job and I worried terribly, we tried very hard not to talk about our problems in front of our boys. We wanted them to live a happy life. I want to mention one small episode that happened in the local department store, BiMart.

I was shopping for something in particular and it was taking me a little bit of time. The boys were browsing through the store when I heard them laughing two rows down from me. I went to see what was so funny and I was not pleased. They found in the plumbing section a very large "plumber's helper." The boys were playing with it and stuck it on the floor in the middle of the aisle. Because of the suction, they couldn't get it off the floor and they were laughing almost hysterically. I started to scold them when a lady clerk walked by, smiled and said to me, "You have nice, healthy and happy boys!" I was surprised that she was not upset and realized that she was right. It was another little piece of the puzzle for me, getting slowly used to the mentality of people who lived in a free society.

Our boys taking any opportunity to have a good time!

23

First Jobs and New Life

Louie finally did come back from Alaska. It was such an awesome moment, seeing him after 14 years. And to think that we thought we would never see each other again. What a twist in our lives! Louie and I spent many long late evenings talking and talking, catching up and on his part, explaining how American society works, what to do and what not to do, what to expect and what not to expect, etc. Louie and the Tomcos wanted to show us McMinnville and the surroundings, including the capital of Oregon, Salem, the biggest city in Oregon, Portland, and 50 miles away, the Oregon coast. This was happening on the weekends. Everything was very exciting for us, but the ocean was the biggest hit. I remember the day when we saw the Pacific Ocean for the first time. I will never forget it, even though the weather was not very pretty – it was in November, wet and windy. Everyone was bundled up. I took off my shoes and jeans and marched into the ocean up to my knees. The water was freezing cold and I couldn't stay for very long. By the way, it was explained to us very quickly that the ocean in Oregon was cold year around. The boys didn't take off any clothes. They started to play a teasing game with the waves and soon got soaked. We ended up in the local laundromat to dry their clothes.

On the weekdays, with Louie's help, I was looking for a job. The first few places we went, he did all the talking. After that he made a statement, "George, this isn't the way to look for a job. You will never get one with me doing all the talking. You must be the one who will introduce yourself and ask for a job, not me." And he was right. I looked everyday. In 1980, the economy was very bad and unemployment was very high. There were not enough jobs even for locals. Louie had taught me one very important sentence that I will never forget. "Hello, my name is George Stastny. I am from Europe – from Czechoslovakia. And I am looking for a job." After I would say this sentence, people would start talking to me. They were very friendly. They would start asking things like, "How do you like America?"

I couldn't understand a word they said. I just wanted to hear "yes" or "no" about the job. I looked for a job everyday from October to January. We were running out of money. It was very, very frustrating. We couldn't stay with Cleo much longer. It was too long to have our family in their house. I remember we had Christmas in their house, and right after that, in January of 1981, I finally got a job. To me it was like hitting the jackpot in the lottery. We moved out of the Tomcos' house immediately and rented a duplex in the same neighborhood.

My new job was in a feed mill – where they ground and cooked the corn and made pellets out of it to feed cows and other livestock. The name of the company was McDaniel Grain and Feed. Two brothers owned this company – Jim and John McDaniel. The title of my job was "mill operator," but it was the worst job you could imagine. However, I was very happy that I finally had a job. The building was huge and was actually a very tall silo with many large bins inside. It didn't look as big from the highway, but believe me, it was very big especially when I was the one who was assigned to keep it clean.

The supervisor took me to a basement that had been accidentally flooded. There was corn dust everywhere three inches deep, on all the equipment, on the huge pipes (12" in diameter), on all the electrical conduits. There were dead, drowned rats just floating there. The water was deep, way over my boots. He gave me a bucket, a broom and a shovel, and said, "Clean it up." I started to work in this mess. I was trying to do my best, and I cleaned it up. When I reported that I had finished, the foreman went to inspect my work, opened his eyes wide and exclaimed, "Gosh, it is clean!" Apparently, other workers had quit after two hours. The foreman told me, "Good job!" I felt that they would keep me working there.

A railroad ran next to the silo where very large railroad cars were brought full of corn and other grain. Unloading was well-mechanized. An underground auger brought corn to the building where there was a grain elevator with a huge, long, vertical conveyor belt. We called this a "belt-evator." The belt had lots of cups that took the corn way above the top of the building for distribution into different pipes going to many large bins. However, there was a problem with one of these distribution pipes. The constant fast-running corn had made a hole in the elbow of the pipe, and the corn, instead of going into the bin, was coming out on the top floor, making a huge mountain. More than half of a railroad car of corn was on the top floor of the grain elevator before the problem was discovered. The corn had to be pushed and shoveled by hand through a small opening (window) into the bin. Guess what??!! This was my next project – to clean up this mess. I knew that this was going to be a lot of hard work, and I knew that I couldn't give up. It was a real test of how much I could take. Even though I was working for minimum wage, $3.25 at that time, I finished this awful job and was totally exhausted. I didn't know if I should be proud of myself or if I was just stupid! They were amazed that I was such a good worker who did not give up.

I would like to share with you what was going through my mind. I was very happy that I had a job because it took me a long time to get it, but when I was working for minimum wage under such difficult conditions – very hard and unpleasant work – I was telling myself all the time, "George, this is not forever. You will reach your dream. Just hang on! Someday, you will have your own business and hopefully, it's going to be in art."

Here is another little story that happened when I was on my way to work one day. I was driving a big old car, a Chevy Impala, on South Davis Street where the speed limit was 25 mph. I was rushing so I wouldn't be late and was going 30 mph. A police officer saw me, stopped me and started to talk to me. I apologized and tried to explain that I don't understand English very well. He asked me, "Do you understand numbers?" I said proudly, "Oh, yes!" Then he replied quickly, "Good. Here is a ticket for $35!" I was not happy. I instantly transferred the $35 to more than one day of hard work. I am very sorry to admit that this was my first speeding ticket but not my last!

I studied English as much as possible and as hard as possible – before I went to work, during work, after work. I was studying hard so I would be able to do more than pushing a broom and a shovel. I wanted to do something better – to be a mechanic, a job for which I was already trained. I couldn't explain what my real experience was or my qualifications. I couldn't explain that I was capable of doing so much more. I could have been a brain surgeon or a space shuttle pilot, but without the language I was just a zero. So, I studied the words for different tools, for different parts of cars and then I was finally able to explain to my employer that I could be a mechanic.

One day the foreman said, "Come with me." He took me to the shop and put me behind a welder and asked if I knew how to use it. I said, "Yes," but I realized it was going to be very different. The metric system is completely different from the U.S. standard system. The pressure gauges on the welder didn't make sense to me. I was familiar with pressure measured in kilograms on a square centimeter. In America, you have pounds on a square inch. So the numbers on the gauges were gibberish to me. I had to estimate the pressure of the torch by the pressure of the flame. I passed the test showing that I could weld and cut with the torch, and the boss was happy. Then he took me to the arc welder. I knew quite a bit about arc welding because I had an arc welder in Czechoslovakia that Simon and I had made from scratch. However, here was another problem – I didn't know about the numbers on the electrodes. We had different numbers in Europe. So I started to weld, and the foreman said, "Wow, this guy can weld anything!" I welded for a couple of hours on different projects and then he said, "OK, now go back to your shovel and broom." Later on I figured out that they were really only testing me. After about a week, they came to me and said, "OK. You are going to be a mechanic now. But you are not going to be working here for Jim. You are going to be working downtown for his brother John, the other owner of this plant." The brothers had two business locations as well as a big farming business. One was the feed mill next to the highway and one was the fertilizer company downtown. John's mechanic at the fertilizer company was retiring. So, they put me in that job. They knew already that I could work – that I was not a quitter or a complainer. When I started as a mechanic, they paid me $4.75. That was very low for being a mechanic, but my English was still very bad, so I was happy to have it.

An interesting story about this downtown fertilizer plant... Several months earlier, when I was looking for work, I had actually knocked on the door of this plant asking for a job. At that time, one of the local farmers by the name of Carl was visiting with John on a business matter. After I left the office (I was turned down for a job), Carl turned to John and said, "That guy isn't just looking for a job. He made an impression on me. He looks like a hard worker and will do things right." Some months later, Jim and John were talking business and John remembered this Czech fellow asking for a job. Jim said, "Yeah, we hired him. He's been working for me at the feed mill, and he knows how to weld and do mechanical work. How about putting him in the fertilizer plant to work for you and to replace the guy who is retiring?" Now, whenever I see Carl, he always remembers that first time meeting me and my horrible English. We laugh about it.

Communicating with my co-workers was always interesting. I will never forget when one time at a staff meeting, John was asking me if I could fix a clutch on one of the company's pickup trucks. I did not know the word "clutch," so I asked in front of everyone, "What is a clutch?" I saw on John's face obvious doubts about what kind of a mechanic I am if I don't know what a clutch is! He was probably thinking, "How can he fix it if he doesn't even know what it is?" But it was a language problem. When I figured out that he meant the part between the engine and the transmission, I said cheerfully, "Oh, 'spojka'! Yes, of course I can fix the clutch – no problem!" People were looking at me and smiling. John was kind of smiling, too, but still shaking his head.

When you are learning a new language, it is a constant, never-ending job on your mind. You are working with a group of people and you don't want to be left out when they tell stories at break time. You want to participate, too. Many times I knew that I could add some good story to the subject that was being talked about. For instance, hunting. I was thinking, "Great! I can tell them my story." So I was putting everything together in my mind to be able to say it with my limited vocabulary. When I was finally ready, they were talking about cars or football. It was very frustrating for me for a long time.

I worked for John McDaniel for 4½ years. I was always asking for a small raise during the first year. He did raise my wages to something like $6.25, but he told me he could not raise it any more and keep me as a year-around employee. He explained that his business was seasonal and that he could only pay me this much and keep me all year. I learned a lot from him, and he was very good to me. I asked him one time if I could fix my car in his shop after hours. He said, "Sure. It's really your shop, George!" I was working on my car, took out the automatic transmission and fixed it even though I had never seen an American transmission before. The boss saw what I did, how I did it, and others saw it. The boss asked if I could fix the transmission on his car. And soon I was working on all the employees' cars. John gave me a key to the shop and let me do all kinds of work in the shop after hours. I remember one Christmas I made a go-kart from extra parts for the boys.

One of my bosses, (I had so many bosses – John, Dick and Jim) Jim, gave me an old, wrecked incomplete frame for a go-kart. I put an old lawnmower motor into it. It wasn't good for racing, but it was a good go-kart for the kids. I made all the missing parts, put everything together the best I could, and then I painted it black and made a bright red vinyl leather-like seat. It looked pretty cool. Other employees were watching my progress and when I was finished they were amazed. "Wow, George, you made a go-kart from

Making a Christmas present for the boys at McDaniel's shop – a go-cart.

An exciting Christmas present for the boys.

nothing!" I said, "Well, it is not the space shuttle. It is just a go-kart." Our boys were very happy to have this Christmas present. We invited many kids from the neighborhood for rides, and they thought it was great. This go-kart meant a lot of good times for lots of kids.

Working for John McDaniel was definitely interesting for me because I was a city boy and he was a farmer. Some of the equipment that I had to work on was totally new to me. I had to use my logic, and I learned a lot about improvising. One of the things that John was involved in was growing grass for seed. This seed needed to be cleaned before it was exported to local farmers as well as all over the world. He bought two used seed cleaning machines ("Clipper" brand made in Wisconsin) at an out-of-state auction and had them shipped to McMinnville. They came in many, many pieces that filled up the whole yard. At first I didn't have any idea what I was even looking at! John came to me and explained that this mess of parts was two seed cleaning machines and said, "I want you to put these together for me. They will be installed in the bottom of this new large building I am constructing to clean grass seed." I was overwhelmed by this responsibility and also the trust he placed in me. I don't want to brag, but on the other hand I am very proud to say that over the next few months, I was able to improvise, figure out what the machines were supposed to look like and what they were supposed to do, and complete the job. These machines were an older system and in the process of assembling them, I was able to use some of the newer technology, which I added to these used machines. These improvements made them comparable to newer equipment.

I would like to bring up another story about the owner, John McDaniel. I never thought that he paid me enough, but on the other hand, he was always very good to me and allowed me to do a lot of things that, I don't think, I would have been able to do somewhere else. One time, I think it was in 1983, John brought an old small outboard motor for a small boat (15 horsepower) to me to fix it. Two weeks after I fixed it, the long Memorial Day weekend was coming. Our family was always involved in any outdoor activities. Helena and I knew how to water ski and both boys knew how to swim. We had a four-person rubber raft with oars. I thought it would be really cool to attach John's small motor onto the rubber raft and go for a cruise on the nearby Hagg Lake. I asked John if he would let me use it. He asked me, "What for?" After I explained it to him, he said, "George, why don't you borrow my big boat and have some real fun this weekend?" I was surprised he would let me use his very nice 22-foot boat. I got very excited, but I quickly started to worry about how I was going to pull it safely. We only had a very small pickup truck. The next day I told John why I couldn't use his boat. His response was awesome, "George, why don't you borrow my big pickup truck along with the boat? That way it will be safe." I was very happy and so was the whole family. We could teach our boys how to water ski, and we had three days of good times on the lake and the river. John was a good guy!

As you know, I had a hard time finding a job, but at about the same time when I finally found my first job, which I just described, the neighbor's daughter came to me with a "Help Wanted" ad in the newspaper for a musician. She knew I could not speak English, but she knew I could play music. The job was in Grizzly Bear Pizza Parlor, and they were looking for a piano player. I remember it like it was today. It was late in the afternoon when I walked in and told the manager my standard line. "Hello, my name is George Stastny. I do not speak English. I am from Europe – from Czechoslovakia, and I am looking for a job..." I also said, "Piano player." He said, "You don't speak English? Well, here is the piano, show us." The pizza restaurant was full of children having a birthday party. I sat down at the piano. I was not a great piano player. I had started to play just for fun when I was in the Air Force. I took a deep breath and started to play. The kids were so, so excited and started to dance to my music and have a good time. The manager came to me and said, "You have the job." I played four nights a week. After the first week, I asked him if I could bring a guitar and banjo and if I could sing. He just looked at me and said, "You don't know how to speak English, how can you sing?" I said, "I know how to speak Czech. I can sing in Czech." He looked at me and said, "OK." So, I brought my guitar and banjo and started to sing American songs in Czech: "Oh, Susanna," "Ghost Riders in the Sky," and many more – but the words were in Czech.

People started laughing and clapping! Most of the time, when you hear musicians playing in a restaurant, most people are not even listening. They're busy eating, drinking, visiting, and the restaurant is quite noisy. It's really hard for a musician to be even noticed under these circumstances. When these people at Grizzly Bear heard songs they recognized being sung with a language they didn't recognize, they were paying more careful attention, and I became exotic to them. I definitely had an advantage since I had contact with my audience. Everybody in town heard the news that there was a Czech piano player and he was playing "Ghost Riders in the Sky" but with Czech words. They could understand only the words "Yippee-yi-ya and yippee-yi-yo." Some people smiled and many people laughed and told me that even on those "English" words, I had an accent. Word got around that there is some really funny musician at Grizzly Bear Pizza. Everyone was saying that you really have to go see him! This went on for two years. Usually a musician stayed in one place for only about 14 days or so. Even people from Portland were coming to see "this Czech musician." The people at the fertilizer plant came and brought their friends. The pizza parlor management was glad to have me there because I was good for business.

I asked the manager, "If I bring George, Jr. on the weekend and he plays the guitar, will you make him a pizza?" George, Jr. was only nine years old at that time. The manager agreed. So I told George, "If you will play for ten minutes, they will make a big pizza for you." George thought that would be very easy and thought ten minutes would go very fast. But when he started to practice, he realized quickly that ten minutes on the stage is a very long time. When he performed, he did well. The place was packed that night and people really liked him. He got so many tips and we also got free food. George, Jr. was on top of the world. He came home with a huge pizza in a box, a full stomach, and some money.

Later, they hired another piano player, a lady, named Mary Ellen. We were playing together for a while. I was playing banjo and guitar, and she was playing piano. She played two days by herself, and I played two days by myself. We didn't see each other very often because we only played one day together. After not seeing me for a while, she tried to give me a compliment, "George, your English is much better." And I said, "Fakt?" which is a very common word in Czech and means "Really?" But to Mary Ellen, with my heavy accent, it sounded like "f..k." Her eyes popped open like tennis balls, "George, you said something very bad!" I was surprised that I had said something that she didn't like. I wanted to know what it meant, how bad it was. She didn't want to tell me and said to ask some of my men friends. I felt absolutely innocent so I asked her one more time. She finally whispered to me, "It means two people, making babies!" Instinctively, I wanted to say again, "Fakt?" but I immediately switched to the English, "Really?" This was only one of many episodes involving learning English.

Playing music in the pizza place was not just important for me because of income, but also for meeting many people who were very friendly. On my breaks or after my performance I was asked to join them at their tables. Even with my limited English at that time, I really enjoyed these conversations because of their friendliness and their intelligence. I met people who

Playing music in Grizzly Bear Pizza Parlor with Mary Ellen.

knew the names of our Czech presidents, Czech cities, landmarks, etc., but occasionally, unfortunately, I also ran into people who were really dumb, asking me questions such as, "Are there cars in Czechoslovakia? Do you have electricity? Have you ever seen a TV?" A couple of these guys went as far as asking me, "Have you ever heard about beer before? Have one and taste it. This is an American beer – Budweiser!" Because of my language barrier, I couldn't let these bozos know how stupid and ignorant they were about my homeland. I wished I could tell them, "If you knew how dumb you sounded, you would be embarrassed! Pilsen was the first lager on the planet, and Budweiser came from Czechoslovakia! Drinking too much beer doesn't make you any smarter!"

Having this job in the pizza place had another advantage. Helena also wanted to have a job and couldn't find one. One day, I met the manager of the local Michelbook Country Club at Grizzly Bear. I found out that they had an open position for a dishwasher so I arranged for Helena to get that job. I wish that it would have been a better job, but what could we do? She was working hard and later, she was allowed to prepare food, which was better than dish washing. Helena and I both can honestly say that we started in America from the VERY BOTTOM!!

I know that I am changing the subject, but I can't forget to tell you about this. When I had worked for John McDaniel about a half a year, my father and my brother were questioned again at Bartolomejska police station. The police were asking my father about my whereabouts. My father played dumb but they got upset with him and started barking, "Don't tell us that you don't know. We know that you know that your son George lives in the U.S. in McMinnville, Oregon. He works as a mechanic for some McDaniel and makes $4.75 per hour!" It was very obvious to me that the police were opening my mail and I found out later that wasn't the only thing they were doing with the mail. From time to time, I put cash in U.S. dollars in these letters to my family, but they never received even one penny.

When I came to America, I didn't have a job, and I couldn't find one. I really worried. But in the next two years I was very busy. I did not know what to do first. I was working full time for McDaniel, and I still played music in the pizza place. I started my own business making large garden planters for landscaping, and I started to sell Kirby vacuum cleaners. Since I was doing demonstrations and selling in people's homes, it was fun to visit with friendly customers. But sometimes it could be a pain in the butt, and I only did this for half a year. I needed all this income very much, because besides supporting my family, we had purchased our first home and had payment obligations.

I would like to talk about the progress of our kids, Martin and George, Jr., and how they adjusted to their new life. It seems to me it was much easier for them than for the adults. First of all, kids in general don't have that much problem learning a new language. They don't even pay that much attention to it. They made new friends in the school and in the neighborhood, and all of a sudden, we realized that they were speaking almost fluently. It was amazing to me.

Frequent family ski trips to Mt. Hood, OR.

The funny thing was that I was the one who had studied English first and very hard, and in the beginning, in McMinnville, helping them with some vocabulary. It was very soon after that when the boys started to correct me, saying, "Dad, you don't say it that way. You need to say it this way!"

I was very proud of both boys for their achievements during that period of their young lives. They were doing fairly well in school and really well in their hobbies. Both boys were constantly creating something with their hands that had wheels or wings. Both of them were into airplane modeling and train sets. Both had jobs delivering newspapers, and I can say they spent all their wages plus some allowance in the local hobby shop.

Display of one of the boys' favorite hobbies at the time – constructing airplanes. Many more were made!

One time, I noticed something negative that I stopped immediately. Some kids in the neighborhood were trading toys between brothers. They were even trying to sell toys to each other that they didn't have an interest in anymore. When I detected this terrible habit in our family between our sons, I got very upset and stopped it immediately. Our sons were looking at me like, "Well, what's wrong with that? It's normal here in America." I explained to them that this is definitely not the way that we are going to operate in our family. I told them, "We will not take advantage of each other and we will be generous to each other because we love each other. If you want to give something to your brother, that is your choice, but don't expect something in return. A generous spirit will always pay off, many times in unexpected ways when you will need it the most." I just couldn't imagine that I would be giving my brother something and asking for money or something else in return. If I got something in return, it was only because of his generosity.

Both boys were constantly on their bikes and skateboards, jumping on them, doing all kinds of tricks, and collecting construction material for making bigger and bigger ramps and half pipes. They were well respected and admired by other kids, and I was very proud of them.

I love to take pictures of our boys having fun. This one was taken at the sand dunes in Florence, Oregon.

I think you would appreciate hearing this story about when our family went on vacation, and we were crossing the border to Canada. If I remember correctly, it was in the summer of 1983. Our plan was to do some camping in Montana and then cross to Canada and eventually visit Vancouver, B.C.

Of course we were not familiar with the area so we were looking at the map and found a border crossing on a two-lane highway that was not busy. We followed the signs to the border and were getting closer and closer. Helena's and my heart started pounding more and more. Please understand this was our first experience leaving the U.S only three years after we had escaped from Czechoslovakia. We finally arrived at the border and saw the big sign saying, "You are leaving the U.S.A." There was a gate on the highway and it was raised. On the left side was also a building that must have been a border patrol office but nobody was around. I stopped the car in front of this raised gate and we were waiting. Nobody came out. After awhile, I got out of the car and knocked on the door of this office. I heard, "Come in!"

I opened the door and stuck my head in. There were two American border officers sitting with their feet on their desks, reading the newspaper. I thought that they were having lunch, and I felt guilty that I was interrupting them. They looked at me and one of them asked me, "What can we do for you?" I replied very politely, "We would like to cross the border, please." The officer kind of leaned to the side so he could see more through the window and said, "The gate is up." He made a face and asked, "What else would you like?" I replied, "I know...uh...uh...would you like to see our documents, our green cards, inspect our car or something?"

I must have looked very shy and confused. Both of these officers raised their eyebrows and started to smile and asked me, "When and where was the last time you were crossing a border?" I replied. "Uh...uh...three years ago leaving Czechoslovakia, going through the Iron Curtain." They responded with friendly laughs and said, "Now we understand!" They got up, shook my hand and said, "This is the U.S.A. You can leave any time but make sure that you have the proper documents to be able to come back." I thanked them, got into the car and we left. Helena was also surprised that nobody was searching our car. We were looking at each other and thinking, "What a country!"

After I had worked for John McDaniel for 4½ years, he and his brother sold the company. It came as a big surprise to all the employees. I remember that it was in the morning about 11:00, when John came to my shop and informed me about the news. He was very apologetic, explaining that my job was guaranteed, but I couldn't be a mechanic, I would have to work with fertilizer. I wasn't interested to work with chemicals and asked him to lay me off, that I would find some job somewhere else. He was trying to change my mind, explaining that the economy wasn't that good, and it would be difficult to find another job. I went to lunch, but instead of eating, I applied for a job in a nearby company, City Sanitary, the local garbage company.

There is a little story that I would like to mention. I walked into the office and introduced myself. The lady working in the office, as I found out later, was Nancy Emrick, the wife of the co-owner and a well-known opera singer. I gave her my job application and explained to her that I was a mechanic and a welder. I explained that I could work on truck engines, transmissions, suspensions and various other equipment. Right at that moment, a foreman of this company walked in. It was Bob Lalonde who I had met at Grizzly Bear Pizza. We saw each other there a number of times, since he was a weekly customer with his church group. He knew me well from there. He asked me what I was doing at the company, and I replied, "I'm applying for a job as a mechanic." He looked at Nancy and said, "George must be a good mechanic. He has done this work for McDaniel for four years, and he is a great musician. He plays piano, guitar, banjo and he's a good singer. The timing is perfect because we need a good mechanic." He looked over my job application and said, "I like this. We will hire you. When can you start?" I replied, "Tomorrow." Nancy was pleased to hear this and responded with a smile and a twinkle in her eye, "George, I like musicians. You just got the job!"

My lunch break was about over, and I had to go back to McDaniel's shop. John came in again, worried about me, and explaining again that I should not be laid off because I would have a hard time getting another job. I said with a smile, "John, don't worry. I know that you mean well, but I just got another job!" He was surprised but wished me good luck.

In the next couple of days, I started to work for City Sanitary and because it was a bigger company, with more mechanics and welders, I was paid $10 per hour. Even though John sold his company, he was still working there as the boss, and he asked me if I could work for him on the weekends and sometimes even after my shift at City Sanitary, repairing farming and other equipment that I was familiar with. I promised I would do my best and as much as I could, but I politely explained that I was getting $10 per hour at City Sanitary. To my surprise, he said, "OK, George. No problem. If you will come and help me, I will pay you $11 per hour!"

I worked for City Sanitary for approximately four years. During this time, the company grew too big so the owners made our division – building garbage handling and processing equipment – a separate company. I was working for this new division as a welder and mechanic. I was able to apply all my experience to this job. At the same time, while working on this specialized equipment, I improved my welding skills and also learned something new.

Most of the time my job was to create "roll-offs," trucks that were able to pull onto their chassis the big garbage drop boxes. When I received a semi-truck, my job was to make the truck a lot longer and install a hydraulic hoist on it. To be able to do that required, literally, to cut the truck in half, including the frame, the driveline, and the electrical, air and hydraulic lines. I had to extend everything, weld it, and put everything back together. It was complicated at first, but later it was just a question of practice. I was also replacing the conventional spring systems with air bags on many trucks. All this work was exciting to me, quite complicated, and I had to apply all my skills to it. I felt I became an even better welder and mechanic.

24

Important Events

During the four years between 1984 and 1988, many important things happened in my life. In 1986, Helena and I got a divorce because of unmanageable differences. I really don't want to talk about the divorce because it was a very painful experience. But to satisfy your curiosity, there was no one else involved. I think that the fault was on both sides, 50-50. Our marriage had become dangerous for all of us, but at the end, we both were able to sit down and make civil decisions. Helena now lives with a Czech fellow in Seattle. I wish her well, but we don't have any contact with each other.

From 1985 to 1987, I was working on getting my U.S. citizenship. In February of 1987, I was officially sworn in as a United States citizen. What an awesome feeling – I could vote, I could have a U.S. passport, I was an AMERICAN!! My co-workers at City Sanitary gave me a surprise party in

Proud U.S. citizen!

our lunchroom. They decorated the room with American flags, and red, white and blue streamers. They had a huge cake made with the whole top decorated with frosting showing the American flag and flowers. Everybody was very happy for me and even sang patriotic songs for me. I was overwhelmed.

Shortly after I became a U.S. citizen, I received two very important welcoming letters. One from President Ronald Reagan and one from Oregon U.S. Senator Bob Packwood. I was very honored. Even though I was officially now a U.S. citizen, I knew I would never forget my background and where I had come from!

Next is a story that really changed my life. At the end of the summer of 1986, I re-met, coincidently, George Jr.'s first teacher, Carolyn Rice. We ran into each other in downtown McMinnville in the bookshop. We hadn't seen each other for two years. After we hugged, I asked her, "Carolyn, what are you doing here? I thought you were somewhere in South America." She replied, "Yes, I'm teaching in Panama. I'm here on my summer leave." We talked for 45 minutes and in the conversation, she asked me if I wanted to see her slide show from the Galapagos Islands, which she had recently visited. I wasn't really interested in pictures of turtles and some blue-footed birds and declined her invitation. After our conversation, we said good-bye, and Carolyn disappeared in the crowd of downtown McMinnville.

I stood there in front of the bookstore thinking I was a real idiot, asking myself these questions, "George, why didn't you ask her where she's staying? You always liked her. She is a great person. She's divorced and so are you. How are you going to find her now?" I was storming my brain for 24 hours, and I figured out the way to find her. I remembered the house where she was helping with a garage sale two years earlier in 1984 just before she left the country for Panama. I armed myself with a lot of courage and knocked on the door of that house. Both husband and wife answered the door, and here I am standing and saying, "Hello, my name is George Stastny. Two years ago you had a garage sale." The couple was looking at me and probably thinking, "We hope he isn't going to return a broken toaster!" I continued, "There was a lady, Carolyn Rice, helping you with the garage sale. I assume that you must be friends with her. I ran into her yesterday in the bookstore, but I forgot to ask her where she's staying. Please, do YOU know?" The lady jumped, smiled and said, "Oh, yes, I know. She's staying with Harriet. I will give you Harriet's phone number!" Her husband was more cautious. He was giving his wife the elbow in the ribs and looking at her like, "You don't know this weirdo!" But it was too late – she gave me the needed phone number.

I went home to call Carolyn but didn't know what kind of excuse I could come up with for the call. When she answered the phone and realized it's me calling, she asked me, "Did you change your mind and you want to come see the slide show?" I replied, halfway surprised and halfway happily, "Oh-oh---oh YES! That's why I'm calling!" I was a lot more interested in Carolyn than in Darwin's discoveries in the Galapagos!

There were at least 20 people seeing these slides, but when the show was over, I was dragging my feet to leave. I was the last to leave the house, and Carolyn walked me to my pickup truck. We talked and talked, leaning against my truck fender for two hours. Before I said good-bye, I asked her if she would go to the beach with me the next day. She accepted and that was our first date. Unfortunately, soon after, she had to return to Panama, and we were dating by mail. The following Christmas we met in Louisiana and spent two weeks visiting hotspots of American music – Nashville for country western, Memphis for blues and rock and roll, and New Orleans for traditional jazz. At that time, I proposed to her and the following April

Our family on top of Mt. Bachelor in the Cascade Mountains in central Oregon – Carolyn, myself and the boys.

of 1987, we were married in Panama. I spent a whole month with her there because I knew she would talk about Panama and her experiences for the rest of her life, and I wanted to be a part of that. And I was right – she does and I gladly help her!

Right after our marriage, both boys decided to live with us full time. Carolyn became an instant mother to two teenagers. She was not a stranger to them since the boys already knew her for years. She was actually George's favorite teacher. My marriage to Carolyn provided the boys with a large extended family with a bunch of uncles, aunts, and cousins with the most important being a grandma and grandpa. After all, everything worked out just fine.

25

Fall of the Iron Curtain and Trips Back

Even though it has been more than 20 years ago, I'm sure that many of you remember well those exciting times when the movement of democracy swept Eastern Europe and the Iron Curtain came tumbling down in 1989. Many of you remember and maybe even saw the Berlin Wall, which was heavily publicized but was actually a very small part of the Iron Curtain. It was not connected to the major parts of the Iron Curtain because Berlin was located in the middle of communist East Germany. The reason for mentioning the Berlin Wall is that many of you remember seeing the news clips on TV and the excitement of the German people on both sides, as they tore down The Wall with sledge hammers and anything else available to them. Unfortunately there wasn't any news coverage of the dismantling of the real Iron Curtain that was over a thousand miles long, dividing free countries from countries under Soviet control.

Communism had finally collapsed! There was nothing more to steal or screw up in those little satellite countries around the former Soviet Union, like Czechoslovakia, Hungary, Poland, East Germany, etc. The Russians had drained them like leeches for more than 40 years, and when those countries were empty, nothing more to steal, then Mikhail Gorbachev said, "Oh, now you can be free!" The world put him on a pedestal, but he was no angel like many people thought.

All Russians and especially their soldiers were close to starving to death. That was an excellent opportunity for Ronald Reagan to deal with Mikhail Gorbachev the way he did. It happened in the summit in Reykjavik in Iceland. Ronald Reagan told Gorbachev to disarm and Gorbachev didn't want to. I saw it like two of the last remaining poker game players. Reagan knew that he had a high hand of cards and also knew that Gorbachev had a very low hand. Reagan insisted on his proposition and didn't budge. Since those two couldn't make an agreement, Reagan returned to the U.S., and I remember his memorable speech to Americans on TV – "Dear fellow Americans. It is better to have no deal with the Russians than a bad deal."

Two weeks later, Gorbachev came back, got on his knees and agreed with Reagan's propositions. And that was the end of the Cold War. People in Czechoslovakia were very happy. Nobody believed that they would be free again in their lifetime. I was following all these developments from here in Oregon, listening to the radio news, reading the newspaper, watching events unfold on the TV, and of course, predicting what should, could and will happen. I even got involved with a public speech in our local Linfield College. The whole world was very excited about these events that moved like an avalanche. Unfortunately everyone was praising and applauding Gorbachev, "Gorby, Gorby, Gorby!" I was trying to tell people that Mikhail Gorbachev was just a communist. I was telling them, "He's not evil, but he would not be so nice if he would have a chance to hold onto communism longer." He was traveling from one Soviet republic to another trying to convince them not to separate from the main Russian republic. But this wasn't possible because, when people get a taste of this much freedom, it is difficult to stop them.

In my opinion, the real heroes who deserve more credit than anyone else for the fall of communism in Eastern Europe were the people who started this movement of democracy. They took a huge risk. They could have been arrested and jailed for life. They had the guts to rise and fight communism, and they were smart and clever to do this in a peaceful way. The first hero is Lech Walesa in Poland and the second is Vaclav Havel in Czechoslovakia. This is not only my opinion – these are the simple facts. Gorbachev helped but only because he didn't stand a chance of stopping this fast moving avalanche of democracy that Walesa and Havel started.

When Czechoslovakia became free, Carolyn and I were very, very happy for its people. For myself, I saw an opportunity to go back and visit my family and friends. But I have to admit, I was very nervous about this idea, and I still worried about my safety. I couldn't imagine that I would be safe there as a former escapee. I contacted my brother, asked a number of questions, and he assured me that there would be absolutely no problem for me to come. I slept on this idea, thought about it carefully, and the result was that in July of 1990, Carolyn and I made an unbelievable and very memorable trip to my homeland. My brother, in the meantime, told EVERYBODY that we were coming. We had a surprise welcoming party at the airport. There were more than 30 people smiling, hugging, kissing and also crying. That trip was really awesome. I think I could write a whole book about that, but I will describe at least the highlights.

First trip back. Carolyn and me under the "Welcome" sign, Prague airport.

Happy reunion with my parents and Carolyn meeting them for the first time.

My parents meeting Carolyn for the first time was one of the biggest highlights. None of us believed that it would ever happen. When they actually met, they were hugging and talking to each other in their own languages. But I knew that no translation was necessary.

We had already been married three years, and my parents were present at our wedding in spirit with the rest of my family and a group of friends. They did something very special for us. Everyone dressed up as if they were going to the wedding (remember, this was 1987 under deep communism plus we were married in Panama) and took several pictures of themselves. We displayed those pictures at our wedding.

I gladly showed Carolyn around Prague, where I was born, grew up and came from. I was able to give Carolyn a tour through my elementary and secondary schools. Another very special highlight was showing Carolyn the house that I built. It was wonderful seeing Czech citizens very happy and talking freely, many of them for the first time in their lives. It was only half

My parents toasting to our marriage.
Translation of the message: "Family and friends of George are greeting family and friends of Carolyn, and we wish Carolyn and George a long life full of happiness! Good Luck!"

Some of my closest friends toasting Carolyn's and my marriage.

a year after the "Velvet Revolution," and everyone was very excited about sharing his or her memorable experiences with us. I was constantly translating for Carolyn. She wanted to talk to people and people wanted to talk to her.

Carolyn and my brother Jaroslav in Prague.

There were many things that I took for granted, but that were unique for Carolyn. She was amazed to see the mail lady going from house to house in this big city of Prague, carrying a bunch of cash in a big leather bag. Remember, I explained earlier that checks didn't exist – everything was done in cash. The mail lady was delivering social security pay to retired people as well as pay to people who were not at work on payday. This lady didn't have any protection such as bodyguards or using an armored vehicle. She was on her everyday route on foot. To be honest, I need to say that this custom soon changed because freedom unfortunately brings negative aspects such as crime.

I need to mention, that until this first trip back to a free Czechoslovakia, I had been having very scary dreams since I had escaped. I had dreams that I was back in Czechoslovakia, and I couldn't get through the Iron Curtain back to the U.S. I frequently cried in my sleep and yelled things in Czech, waking Carolyn who then had to wake me up. What a relief when I realized that it was only a dream! An interesting thing is that these dreams stopped after this first trip and the realization that the Iron Curtain was really gone, and it was safe for me to go back and forth.

Many friends and family greeting us at the airport – the first trip back for the boys.

After this first trip, we immediately made a new plan to go back and take the boys with us. Two years later we did just that. It was another joyful experience from start to finish. When Martin and George, Jr. left the country in 1980, they were just little boys. When we brought them back, they were 19 and 21. What a big difference for them in that stage of their lives. We had another welcoming committee, with lots of tears from friends and relatives. Martin's and George's cousins were also young adults, and it was so much fun witnessing this joyful reunion. They had so much to explain and talk about.

Martin and George, Jr. catching up on many years with cousins.

Surprisingly, even though they really hadn't practiced, the boys still remembered their Czech language, although their vocabulary had remained that of seven and nine-year-olds. The Czech cousins had a lot of laughs listening to their cute childish speech. Everywhere we went we saw people talking and showing with their hands, "I remember you when you were this tall, and now you are this tall!" This reconnection of the boys and their relatives, especially the cousins, was accompanied by lots of hugs from the time we arrived to the time our plane took off for the U.S.

Now I believe that it would be a good time to mention something that you would appreciate knowing. Over a number of years, my wife, Carolyn, and I have gone back to Czechoslovakia on numerous occasions. It was always enjoyable visiting with the people who had helped me with my escape. We thought at the time, that we would never see each other again. The first

Cousins! From left: Martin, Jolana, George, Jr., Roman.

George, Jr. on left, Martin on right with more of the cousins.

reunion with my friends Simon and Jaroslav Zeman was big and very happy! We certainly had a lot to talk about.

But there was another person that I will never forget and I was thinking about a lot and always wanted to see again. That person was Vasek Schuster in Vienna, the one who didn't hesitate to help a stranger – me. Over the years I had lost contact with him because he moved. I searched for him, and I found out that he was still in Vienna but had bought a house in a different location. In 2005, during a trip back to Prague, Carolyn and I made a plan to visit him in Vienna. We were taking a driving trip from Prague to Vienna.

When we stopped overnight in Moravia, we got a phone call from Carolyn's father that her mother was very ill and would not live much longer. We called Vasek, explained the situation, turned around, got on the plane in Prague, flew to the U.S. and were able to see her before she passed away.

In 2009, Carolyn and I were again traveling through Europe and we were finally able to see Vasek in Vienna. It had been 29 years since I saw him last. We both wondered if we would recognize each other. I even made a big sign with my name on it. Seeing him again was just awesome.

Vasek Schuster, friend from Vienna, toasting our reunion after 29 years.

For my wife Carolyn, it was exciting meeting him since she had heard so much about him. He picked us up in downtown Vienna and took us to his house. His wife, Vera, was waiting for us and the excitement was high. She made a wonderful meal, and we talked and talked until midnight. Vasek hadn't changed much – he was still a good-hearted friend. We extended an invitation to visit us in the U.S. and hope that someday that will happen. I would be so happy to repay even a little token of my thanks to them.

As I mentioned in the very first page of this book, I'm not a book writer, and I asked you to be patient because I knew that telling the long and complex story would have many sidetracks. Well, here is another one.

I was very happy to be in this country, being a U.S. citizen, and I wanted to celebrate my ten-year anniversary and invite all the people who helped me when I first came to McMinnville. I always wanted to acknowledge the help that my family and I received from many different people when we were going through the first difficult times of starting our new life in the U.S. I made a list of these people and shortly after we returned from our first trip back to Prague, in October of 1990, all of them were invited with their spouses to our house. We gave these wonderful people a big party as a thank you for their help and generosity. I enjoy designing business cards and brochures for my business, so I was thinking for a while what the invitation to this party should look like. I came up with an attractive graphic that stated with big letters "10 Years" with the lettering looking like the U.S. flag along with little red hearts. I ordered a large cake from the bakery in our local supermarket and had them do the exact same design on the top of the cake. When I was picking up the cake, all the bakery employees came to see me. They were very happy and excited for me and were giving me compliments

It is my pleasure to invite you to a 10th Anniversary Party. It seems like yesterday when, on October 6, 1980, my family and I arrived in the United States and came directly to McMinnville. There were some major changes and adjustments in my life and many problems. But there were also many good people like you, and they didn't hesitate to help. You didn't help me just to establish myself in this country and community, but you did a lot more. You became dear friends, and thanks to you, I find this place my home.

George

"10 Years" party invitation.

that they liked seeing someone who appreciated being in this country. They told me so many people take for granted being here. I was pleased to see these bakers showing their enthusiasm. I often remind people living in this country that they should not deprive themselves of such a great feeling to be able to live in such a beautiful country, to belong to it, and to be FREE!

When the party started, I introduced each person individually, and it was interesting to watch people's reactions. It was really enjoyable for everybody. Many people didn't know each other, but all of them knew me, and all of a sudden, it felt like seeing a large group of people finishing a gigantic jigsaw puzzle together. I heard people say, "Oh yes! Now I know who you are! I heard about you a number of times from George! It's such a pleasure meeting you!" And I knew that they meant it.

My sponsors and very good friends, Ed and Cleo Tomco.

I would like to mention the names of a few people who were invited. Besides our family members, the list included my sponsors and honored guests, Ed and Cleo Tomco; my friend Louie (he couldn't come since he was living in Alaska); the pastor of the church, Doug Rose, who put out the call for someone to offer me a job; the logger, Don Endicott, who agreed to sign the paperwork certifying that I would have a job; my former employers John McDaniel of McDaniel Feed and Seed and Ezra Koch of City Sanitary; Roger Egan, my dentist, who cared more about my teeth than about my paying him; Terry Crow from the insurance company who helped me compose letters and flyers to prospective clients when my English wasn't very good; the owners of the printing company, Thelma and David Vanbergen, who were very patient with me when I was having my brochures printed; and many other people. I became friends with these people and we are still friends today.

26

A Special Flag

Just before Carolyn and I left for home from our first trip back to
Czechoslovakia, one of my friends, Ivan Votava, found out that Carolyn's
father, Col. Keith Sherman, was a WWII veteran. Ivan surprised us with a
very unique and precious gift for Carolyn's father and other U.S. veterans
– a large homemade and hand-sewn American flag. This flag was sewn
overnight in 1945 to welcome the U.S. Army that was liberating the western
part of Czechoslovakia. Ivan also wrote a heart-felt thank you letter to go
with the flag that I translated into English. I have to admit that this was a
very emotional experience translating this letter. Ivan got the flag from an
old farmer who had it secretly hidden in his barn since the end of WWII.
I always knew, but Carolyn didn't, that many Czech people had treasures

Carolyn's father, Col. Keith Sherman, receiving special flag for U.S. veterans.

hidden away to honor the liberation by U.S. troops on Czech soil. But these treasures had to be hidden from the communists. These were artifacts that had been collected and saved after the liberation was over and the Americans had left Czech soil. Even large items like jeeps and trucks were buried under straw and haystacks inside barns. Ivan received this special flag as a gift for a favor he did for an old farmer. Here is the text of the letter he wrote:

To the War Veterans of the United States of America who helped to liberate Czechoslovakia in 1945:

Dear Friends,

Forty-five years ago in May, 1945, your United States Army under the command of General Patton, liberated West Bohemia and the city of Pilsen.

Thanks to the horrible communist system, these facts were deliberately withheld and people were forced to "admit" that all of Czechoslovakia was liberated by the Soviet Union only. This disgusting system went so far as to remove all monuments and memorials to the American soldiers who died in the liberation process. The communist government persecuted people who put flowers in these places in remembrance and honor to your soldiers who couldn't return to their homes.

From the bottom of my heart, I would like to apologize to all of you for this inconceivably ugly ideology. At the same time, please accept a small gift. It is an American flag that welcomed American soldiers in May of 1945 in Pilsen. This flag was homemade instantly during the liberation and sewed in a hurry. I believe that you will understand and excuse a little mistake of six-pointed starts. I obtained this flag 15 years ago, and I have guarded it since then. All these years when this flag couldn't billow, it finally flew this spring in the place of its birth, Pilsen, and in Prague, the place where I live. I think that the time has finally arrived for this flag to get into the hands that it was originally made for.

I wish you all very good health and much personal happiness. I hope that someday I can welcome you on the soil of our free country.

Sincerely,
Ivan Votava
Prague, August 6, 1990

When Carolyn and I got back to Oregon, we called Carolyn's father and told him that we had a special gift for him, but that we weren't going to give it to him right away because we wanted to use it for awhile. Carolyn and I made a number of patriotic presentations with the centerpiece of the speeches being this special flag. The response was overwhelming with people being very moved by what they saw and heard and about such a long-lasting friendship of the Czech people with Americans.

During our presentations, I was realizing that I should send some kind of nice present to Ivan as a gesture of repayment for his gift to American veterans. I thought about this carefully for a long time and then, finally, I had the wildest idea to send him another American flag, but this time, a real American flag that had been flown over the U.S. Capitol building. The challenge was how to get this flag. I remembered that when I became a U.S. citizen, I received two welcoming letters as I mentioned previously, one from President Reagan and one from our U.S. senator from Oregon, Bob Packwood. At the end of Sen. Packwood's letter, he had mentioned that if I ever needed anything, that I was welcome to contact his office.

I composed a letter that explained in a short version the situation with this special American flag. I respectfully asked if Sen. Packwood could provide me with a replacement flag that had been flown over the U.S. Capitol. I was very pleased when the response came from Washington, DC that the senator would be happy to provide a flag along with a certificate stating its authenticity, dedication to Ivan Votava and the date it was flown. Sen. Packwood also told me that he would be happy to present this flag to me in person, in our home in McMinnville so he could also see the original flag from WWII. This was very good news because I thought immediately that it would be a good time to invite Carolyn's father. The special flag could be presented to him in the name of WWII American veterans at the same time the new flag for Ivan was presented to me.

When the local media found out about this event, representatives came to our house to report and photograph the exchange of these two special flags. An excellent picture was taken in our back yard of both flags being held side by side by Sen. Packwood and Col. Sherman. Seeing these two flags displayed like this allowed us to compare them, and you could see the differences. In their haste to create a flag to welcome the liberating troops, the Czech seamstresses didn't know the correct proportions of the red and white stripe field to the blue field, nor did they know the stars should be five points instead of six. Knowing this makes their effort even more special.

Both special flags side by side. On left, flag sewn in a hurry in 1945 to welcome U.S. troops. On right, flag flown over U.S. Capitol. From left, Col. Sherman, Carolyn, U.S. Senator Bob Packwood, myself.

When the flag was finally in the hands of Carolyn's father, he was also very moved and continued with presentations to many veterans' groups and other military circles. I know from what Carolyn's father told me, that every veteran and soldier who was in attendance at these presentations saluted this flag.

The story about this flag was published in our local newspaper and got even more publicity. I translated the story into Czech and included this with the newspaper article and the new flag that I sent to Ivan. I thought this was basically the end of the story on my part. But then several months later, I received a letter from Ivan, which included a brand new story from the Czech newspaper in Prague. I was very pleased to know that so many people in both countries found out about these two flags, which showed again the friendship between the Czechs and the Americans.

After Carolyn's father, Col. Sherman, was finished with his presentations using the special flag, both of her parents drove to Ft. Knox, Kentucky, to the General Patton Museum. The flag was officially presented and dedicated to all American veterans and is on display there today. The last thing I needed to do was to respond to a request from the Gen. Patton Museum. I was asked to testify in writing how I received this flag, where and from whom, and to include Ivan's original letter to U.S. veterans.

27

Starting My Dream Business

I would like to dedicate this last chapter to describing the business that I started in 1981, an art business making pots. I saved this for last on purpose. I was occupied with this business all these years, dedicating more and more of my time to it. I didn't want to constantly interrupt my story describing the progress of my own business, so now, I can talk about this in one piece, hopefully briefly and descriptively.

Each piece is individually hand-carved and chiseled.

I combined all my skills, experience and love of art and started to make large planters and fountains for decorating landscaping projects. I saw a need and a potentially good market for this garden art. I hand-carved and chiseled these planters out of a special mix that I developed. The material is like concrete, very hard, heavy, durable and attractive. Every piece has thick walls, reinforced with circles of rebar that I weld together. All of my designs were very successful and some of them became very popular. This helped business tremendously.

By 1987, I was dedicating so much time to this work that I couldn't keep up with my other jobs. For that reason, I had to quit them one by one, and I committed myself completely to making pots.

I called my creations "pots" because my English was somewhat limited at that time. Over the years, many customers have asked me to find a fancier terminology for my vessels other than "pots," but for the sake of tradition and simplicity, I am still using the name "Stastny Stone Pots." In the beginning, I started to do my business in a single car garage. I didn't have a pickup truck so I brought material to my "studio" in the trunk of the car. When my business grew out of this small space, I had to rent a larger shop in Yamhill, a nearby town. Another reason for moving out of the single car garage was the divorce with Helena – I had to move out. When Carolyn and I got married in 1987, we bought a small house (900 sq. feet, two small bedrooms and one bath) in a secluded residential area south of McMinnville. It was especially small for a family of four because both boys were living with us fulltime. At that time they were already 14 and 16. Since this house had a double garage, I moved all my business into it.

My art work, in front of customer's home, showing one of many designs.

My desire to be an artist, to have my own studio, and to be successful, meant that I had to also promote my business with informational literature. I used my skills in photography, graphic design and drawing, and created business cards, brochures and portfolios. I promoted and advertised my business everywhere, as much as I could, introducing myself to hundreds, maybe thousands of landscape architects and designers, in person, over the phone and in the mail throughout the United States and Canada. I was exhibiting my work in many large and elegant home and garden shows as well as international and nursery trade shows. I met and became friends with the owners of some of the most successful and beautiful nurseries on the continent. These relationships proved very useful and helpful.

Front cover of my latest brochure. Brochures entirely redesigned about every three years. This edition contains 50 colored pictures of my various designs.

As my business was growing, I had a need again for a larger studio to accommodate bigger equipment for making larger pots. So I built a new shop building next to our house on the empty lot. At that time, I was already well known which is extremely important for an artist. I had been featured many times in various newspapers, magazines, on major TV stations and in many Street of Dreams projects. Most of my work was purchased for private homes and some for high-end commercial projects. I started to make much bigger pots, up to five feet in diameter, which weighed 3,500 pounds. I was also making 13-foot tall formal fountains and large informal cascading fountains. Of course these pieces required heavier equipment. I had to purchase larger hoists, forklifts, pickup trucks, trailers and hydraulic tailgates. My business grew to a scale that I couldn't operate it out of my shop in a residential area anymore. My wife and I purchased three acres of property, nine miles west of our home with 900 feet of highway frontage. Here, on this busy highway, I started to build my dream garden gallery and Stastny studio. I did as much as I could by myself, just like I built my house in Czechoslovakia from scratch. It took just about the same time, six years. I still needed to hire an excavating contractor and part-time labor help.

I need to tell you about something that made me feel good, and I hope that it will also make you feel good. Landscaping of this property was very extensive and, of course, expensive. I had been collecting hundreds of large, beautiful, and rare mature plants. I had them temporarily stashed in one place in bark and sawdust so I could water them easily. In the meantime, I was working hard on the landscaping, preparing various garden areas, creating walkways for customers to be able to move easily throughout the whole gallery. The time was quickly coming to plant all the trees and shrubs in their permanent spots. I needed to do this fast, and since the whole landscaping project was very expensive, I worried that I wouldn't have enough money to hire extra workers to help me. I shared my worries with Carolyn and she advised me, "Why don't you ask our friends to help you? If they won't come, then worry." I asked 18 friends to help and guess what? Seventeen people showed up and we planted 200+ plants in one weekend! Since some of these were blooming rhododendrons, the whole gallery was instantly beautiful! It was a great work party and an unforgettable experience. We are very lucky to have friends like that!

Eventually, I also hired a contractor to build my new and much larger shop, 36 by 60 feet. I moved my entire business to the new shop and gallery. This new shop was very nicely equipped. It was endless and exhausting hard work, but it paid off. The Stastny Gallery is exclusively and exquisitely landscaped and has become a well-known landmark.

Customers enjoy strolling through the gallery any time of the year.

Besides my own work, I also started to represent other artists. In my office, I have on the wall a map of the U.S. and Canada with a countless number of colorful pins covering the entire continent (except Mexico) showing where my work is located. The walls are also covered with many winning plaques and ribbons that I received for displaying my work at various shows. One plaque that I treasure the most is the award for "Beautification of Our County." There is also a framed and personally signed (for me) picture of President Ronald and Nancy Reagan.

Over the years, I have become a highly respected member of our business and private community. I've become personal friends with all my former employers, with influential figures of our community (doctors, lawyers, business owners, civic leaders) and with elected leaders (mayor, sheriff, commissioners, Congressional representatives, etc.). It is a great pleasure for me to be invited to high-class functions, be well-recognized and feel welcome. I've heard a couple of times, when I was being introduced, "George is our American Dream success story. He came here in 1980 with a suitcase, didn't speak English, worked hard and look at him now!"

What I'm personally proud of the most is when I finished building the Stastny Gallery, opened it for business, and raised the American flag for the first time! My dream had come true. I am an ARTIST, with my own GALLERY, and a large American FLAG flying over it!

And that is the whole story.

Dear readers and fellow Americans, my thanks go to all of you!

Questions for Discussion

- How would you have reacted if faced with the same situation which George encountered?

- If your spouse, or significant other, decided that it was necessary to flee your homeland and immigrate to a completely foreign country, with an unknown language and culture, how would you respond?

- George fled in 1980. The Iron Curtain came down in 1989. In what ways do you think George's actions would have been different had he known his country would have been opened nine years later? Do you think he would have fled anyway?

- What parallels, if any, do you see between George's life and yours?

- Do you think George is fair in his assessment of the political climate he experienced?

- Which parts of the story do you find most inspiring?

- Which parts of the story do you find most upsetting in terms of possible occurrence in our country?

- In your own life, what extreme life-changing circumstances have you encountered?

- If you had an opportunity to meet George, what would you like to ask him about his life?